Travellers Wine Guide

France

To Ralph and Denise, inveterate vineyard visitors.
May they and many others find this book of use in their travels.

Travellers Wine Guide

France

Christopher Fielden

Photographs by Michel Brioul
and Janet Price

WAYMARK

The *Travellers Wine Guides*
were conceived and produced by
Philip Clark Limited
53 Calton Avenue, London SE21 7DF, UK

Designed by Keith Faulkner Publishing
Limited

Edited by Philip Clark

Photographs by Michel Brioul and
Janet Price (except where otherwise
credited)

Maps by Andrew Green and Simon Green

Published in Great Britain by
Waymark Publications, an imprint of
the Automobile Association, Fanum House,
Basingstoke, Hampshire RG21 2EA

© Philip Clark Limited, 1989
First published 1989

ISBN 0 86145 761 7

Phototypeset in Great Britain by
Input Typesetting Limited

Colour reproduction in Singapore by
Columbia Offset Limited

Printed and bound in Hong Kong

PHOTO CREDITS

Michel Brioul half-title, 6/
7, 15, 18, 19, 20, 21, 22/23,
23, 26, 28, 29, 30, 31, 32,
33, 40, 41, 42, 50/51, 53,
54, 55, 57, 58(2), 61, 62, 64,
65, 66, 68, 70, 71, 72, 74,
78, 79, 83, 84, 87, 90, 91,
92, 94/95, 97, 99, 100, 101,
102, 103, 104, 105, 107,
108, 109, 111, 114, 115, 116,
117, 118, 119, 120, 124/125
(bottom), 126

Janet Price 12/13, 14, 25,
34, 36, 38, 38/39, 44, 45,
46, 47, 48, 49, 52, 60, 69,
73, 85

**Comité Inter-
professionnel des Vins
d'Origine du Pays
Nantais** 86

**Comité Inter-
professionnel des Vins de
Touraine** 81

**Food and Wine from
France** 133

**French Government
Tourist Office** 128

Francesco Venturi 16

Zefa Picture Library
jacket, 122, 124/125(top)

Contents

How to Use this Book

This book is designed for the tourist, especially the motorist, who wants to see how wine is made, to taste it and, possibly, to buy it. While wine can be bought in shops, and tasted in restaurants, in France it is the cellars that count.

In some towns – Beaune is a notable example – there are a number of shops specializing in the sale of the local wines. For the most part, however, French people buy their wine in supermarkets, or direct from the grower. Their contact with a grower may be through a representative who will come to the door with samples. It may be by an annual visit to the vineyard to talk and to taste. It may be by buying at one of the many regional Fairs, where there will be wine-stands.

Visiting vineyards

This book is mainly about vineyard visiting, though a number of local wine fairs are listed, with approximate dates. These are wonderful events for tasting and comparing, though the chances of purchasing more than the odd bottle or two on the spot are small, as most of the orders taken are for subsequent delivery. This is a method of buying wine that I would not recommend. Direct importation is best left to the professionals.

As you are driving through France, you can dip into the book to find basic information about the local wines, the names and addresses of some of the local growers and merchants and places of interest, such as wine museums. For most areas, too, there is the address of the office of the body looking after the promotion of the local wines. Here they will probably have available complete lists of local growers and detailed wine maps of the region.

Tourist offices

I can also recommend a visit to the local tourist office and addresses are given of many of these in the wine regions (see page 140). They are invariably helpful and they can usually come up with some individual or topical advice. Alternatively, if you wish to know about the basic driving regulations in France, how many gallons a grower produces when he talks in litres or the best way of buying wine to bring home, it is all here in the book.

Wine touring

While this book is designed to be as self-contained as possible, it cannot take the place of a road atlas. For detailed maps showing short cuts or scenic routes, I would suggest that the wine-loving motorist also buys the Michelin Road Atlas.

One of the pleasures of wine touring is the limitless interest of the subject. Each year the wine is different, each season the scenery changes. Round every corner there is a new grower or merchant to be visited.

This book will give you an introduction to just a few of them. It is a beginning, but by no means the whole. I hope that for the newcomer to vineyard visiting it will open the first doors and, for the hardened regular, it will provide some new addresses.

There can be few more satisfying ways of passing time in France than to talk to a grower about his wine, with a glass of it in your hand. I hope that this book will help you to achieve this satisfaction.

Information panel symbols

E	English spoken
TF	tastings are free
TP	tastings must be paid for
WS	wine for sale
t	telephoning in advance advisable
T	telephoning in advance essential

Note

Where practicable, it is a good idea to contact the grower in advance of a visit, not only out of politeness, but also to check that nothing has changed since the information in this book was compiled. (See the notes on how to use a French telephone, and the model letter in French, on page 141.)

Foreword _____

The first visit that I made to the vineyards of France on my own was in 1958, when I was eighteen and I had just started in the wine trade. I visited the National Wine Fair at Mâcon and humbly presented myself, with a letter of introduction, at the office of Monsieur Jean Mommessin, who was the chairman of the Fair. I think my real love of wine dates from the welcome that I was given then.

Every year since, I have been back to France, which for me is the most satisfying of all wine countries to visit. For the British motorist, the Channel is but the threshold to be crossed, and for the visitor from further away, such well-known vineyards as Champagne and Chablis are less than two hours from Paris.

I hope that this book will open doors for its readers to the countless pleasures that I have had from the vineyards and cellars of France.

The walled cité *(Old Town) of Carcassonne, in south-eastern France, viewed across a green sea of vines. The mediaeval ramparts were painstakingly restored in the 1840s by Viollet-le-Duc.*

Introduction _____

Frace is not the world's largest producer of wine, nor does it have the largest area under vines. Those distinctions belong to Italy and Spain respectively. Nevertheless, it is to France that the consumer tends to look for quality. This is true not only in Britain, where out of every ten bottles of wine drunk, almost four come from France, but in almost every country in the world.

This is no coincidence, for it is in France that the broadest variety of wines is made. You can find every style of wine there if you are prepared to look for it: not just the classic wines of Bordeaux and Burgundy, but also such rarities as Château Chalon from the Jura, which rivals the finest fino sherry.

There is always something new to see and taste, and there can be no more hospitable vocation than that of wine producer. Whether you speak French or not, if you are interested in the end product, the producer will make you welcome.

This book should be particularly helpful to the motorist who is interested in visiting some of the vineyards of France while he is driving through, as it is based on the motorway system, which radiates out from Paris in all directions.

Many of the most important wine regions lie close to the motorways - who can forget the first sight of the vineyards of Burgundy when the A6 swoops down on the town of Beaune?

With the help of this book, you can choose where to leave the main roads to break off and spend as little or as much time as you like, with glass in hand talking to the grower about his wines.

I do not know how many hundreds of thousands of wine-makers there are in France. This book can only give but a small selection. The choice has been mine – but each has said that he will make visitors welcome. Some are no more than individual growers who might perhaps work the soil and make the wine with no more help than that of their immediate family. Some are multinational companies whose brands are household names around the world and whose cellars welcome hundreds of thousands of visitors each year. I must admit that I have tried to avoid the 'tourist traps', of which there are some in every vineyard region. Even in areas where the big brands dominate, like Champagne and Cognac, I have included some smaller family businesses.

A voyage of discovery

Vineyard-visiting is a voyage of discovery. In researching this book I have been to places that I have never been to before and I have made a host of new friends. I hope that readers, too, will discover much. There can be no country that has as broad a range of wines as France and it is often away from the well-beaten paths that the most pleasure is to be had.

Dunkerque
Calais
Boulogne
Lille
Cherbourg
Dieppe
Amiens
Le Havre
Rouen
Caen
R. Seine
Brest
Paris
Reims
Metz
Rennes
CHAMPAGNE
R. Marne
Nancy
Strasbourg
Troyes
Blois
ALSACE
Nantes
R. Loire
Tours
Chablis
Colmar
LOIRE
CHABLIS
R. Saône
SANCERRE AND
POUILLY-SUR-LOIRE
Chalon-sur-Saône
JURA
R. Chatente
BURGUNDY
COGNAC
SAVOIE
Bordeaux
R. Rhône
Lyon
BORDEAUX
R. Dordogne
Grenoble
R. Garonne
RHONE
Bayonne
Pau
Toulouse
Avignon
Montpellier
Nice
LANGUEDOC-
ROUSSILLON
PROVENCE
Marseilles
Perpignan

The System of Classification

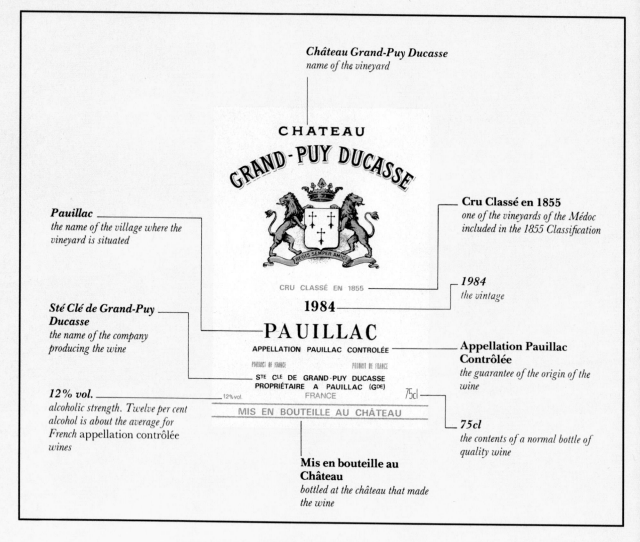

Château Grand-Puy Ducasse
name of the vineyard

CHATEAU
GRAND-PUY DUCASSE

Pauillac
the name of the village where the vineyard is situated

Cru Classé en 1855
one of the vineyards of the Médoc included in the 1855 Classification

CRU CLASSÉ EN 1855

1984
the vintage

Sté Clé de Grand-Puy Ducasse
the name of the company producing the wine

1984

PAUILLAC

APPELLATION PAUILLAC CONTROLÉE

PRODUIT DE FRANCE   PRODUIT DE FRANCE

Sᵀᴱ Cᴸᴱ DE GRAND-PUY DUCASSE
PROPRIÉTAIRE A PAUILLAC (Gᴰᴱ)
12% vol.   FRANCE   75cl

MIS EN BOUTEILLE AU CHÂTEAU

Appellation Pauillac Contrôlée
the guarantee of the origin of the wine

75cl
the contents of a normal bottle of quality wine

12% vol.
alcoholic strength. Twelve per cent alcohol is about the average for French appellation contrôlée wines

Mis en bouteille au Château
bottled at the château that made the wine

All the wines of France are classified according to a rigid hierarchy, depending on the potential quality of the wine. At the bottom comes the simple *vin de table*. This may come from anywhere in France and is generally blended from a variety of sources, mainly from within France itself, though other wines made in the Common Market can be blended in if the fact is mentioned on the label. This is the wine for everyday drinking, sold in plastic bottles or the ubiquitous, returnable, six-star litre bottles. It will have no vintage, and the label will generally give no more than a brand name and the alcoholic degree of the wine.

Vins de Pays
One step up the ladder come the *vins de pays*. For these wines there are strict controls on the quantity that may be produced per hectare, the grapes that are used and their source. The region of production may be quite small, for example, the Vin de Pays des Coteaux de Peyriac; from

one *département*, like a Vin de Pays de l'Aude; or from an even wider area like a Vin de Pays du Pays d'Oc.

Occasionally there are surprises to be found when a grower will experiment with a classic grape variety where it has not previously been grown. Particular examples are the Cabernet Sauvignon, the Chardonnay and the Syrah. Such wines can now be found in the Midi and the Rhône valley.

Superior quality wines

Higher up the scale come V.D.Q.S. wines. The letters stand for *Vin Délimité de Qualité Supérieur* (superior quality wine). These are sometimes traditional regional wines, like the acid rosé wines of Lorraine called Côtes de Toul, and sometimes wines that are progressing up the ranks. Here the controls on production are more strict – and the prices higher.

At the top of the ladder come the *appellation contrôlée* wines. I say at the top of the ladder, but there one finds a broad platform, which will include wines that have recently been promoted from V.D.Q.S. status, like Minervois, and some of the greatest and most expensive wines in the world, like Romanée-Conti from Burgundy.

The label

Whatever the French wine, its classification will appear on the label. Thus you can tell easily where it stands in the classification scale. A word of warning, however: the rating is not necessarily related to quality, but more to the controls that have been made on the production. It is possible to find excellent, and expensive, *vins de table*. Perhaps the vineyard is the wrong place, perhaps

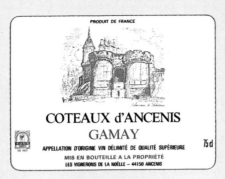

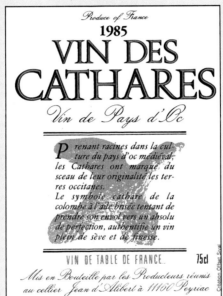

Vin Délimité de Qualité Superieure (V.D.Q.S.)
The special seal for this category of wine appears in the bottom left-hand corner of the label. Also shown is the grape variety from which it is made – the Gamay. The Coteaux d'Ancenis are on the north bank of the River Loire, just to the east of Nantes.

Vin de Pays
This is still a table wine, but it comes from a specific region, the Pays d'Oc, or Languedoc. The label also gives the vintage.

Vin de Table
The source of the wine is shown simply as France. The strength of the wine is shown in the bottom right-hand corner. As this is a sweet wine, the label gives not only the alcoholic degree, but also the potential strength that would be added if the residual sugar were fermented out.

the vines are too young or the grape variety is not accepted in the region.

Surely, here lies one of the real attractions of visiting the growers – the opportunity of discovering a wine that belies its status. Good hunting!

Travelling in France

SPEED LIMITS
Urban areas 60kph/37mph
Normal roads 90kph/
56mph: (in wet) 80kph/
49mph
Dual carriageway 110kph/
68mph: (in wet) 100kph/
62mph
Motorway 130kph/80mph:
(in wet) 110kph/68mph

The open road. Libre service on the garage means self-service. Note the difference in price between the fuels; super and ordinary petrol – and diesel.

Travelling in France

For the most part, motoring in France is not difficult. There is a broad motorway system that can enable considerable distances to be covered in a short time. On the motorways, there are frequent parking places to rest and numerous restaurants where one can eat and drink reasonably.

The cost of motorway tolls can mount up, however, and, if speed is not important, there are generally main roads which run in parallel. These can to be crowded with heavy vehicles. In any case, all roads are to be avoided at the beginning and end of holiday periods, even holiday weekends, as traffic jams appear to be endemic. Alternative long-distance routes are marked with green signs.

Petrol

Petrol is expensive in France and of two qualities. Most cars run on Super. Diesel, on the other hand, is up to 30 per cent cheaper. Generally, a great deal of money can be saved by filling up at a hypermarket; all of them have petrol pumps, though credit cards are often not accepted. Although, in theory, Eurocheques are widely accepted for payment, many

service stations, particularly privately-owned ones, are reluctant to accept these because of delays in clearing them.

Car hire

For those arriving in France without a car, and hoping to hire one, a word of warning: hire-cars are liable to a luxury rate of value added tax and can become very expensive. It might well be worthwhile to hire one just across the border.

Hotels

Hotels are for the most part not expensive, though the bedrooms can be somewhat spartan. The Logis de France is a chain of independent family-run hotels. They are generally reasonably priced, clean and comfortable. There are also a number of chains of simple hotels, generally on the approaches to towns, which can be ideal for one-night stopovers with all rooms having private baths and television. They also have clean, friendly restaurants, often with a buffet *hors d'oeuvres*, and simple grills as main courses. Three such chains with hotels all over France are Ibis, Campanile, and Climat de France.

Finally, it is always wise to book your hotels in advance.

Driving in France

Here are a few simple rules about driving in France. Driving is on the right and priority is on the right. In the open countryside, main roads always have priority, but beware of cars leaping out from the right in town.

Until recently, cars coming into a roundabout always had priority, therefore often leading to a position of stalemate. This is now changing and there will be clear signs saying if you now do not have priority.

Carry a full driving licence, vehicle registration document and evidence of insurance cover. A Green Card is not always necessary, but for full cover you should have one. Consult your insurer.

Hazard warning lights or a red warning triangle and a spare set of bulbs must be carried.

Seat belts must be worn in the front of a car and children under ten must not travel in the front, except in a two-seater car.

An accident causing injury must be reported to the police and, after any other accident involving someone else, an accident report form should be filled in.

Spot fines of up to about £90 ($150) can be imposed by the police for speeding and drink-driving offences. In the latter case, the car can be impounded. This can also happen if you cannot pay the fine in cash. Cheques are not acceptable. Random breath tests occur, so do not consider driving after too serious cellar visits!

Visiting a Winery

Each visit suggested in this book will have its own particular character. and this may vary from day to day. Some wineries particularly ask visitors to telephone in advance, in a few cases days in advance. These are probably growers who are arranging to take time off from their work in the vineyards or the cellars to welcome you. They are not equipped to receive large parties. If, for any reason you are unable to keep your appointment, or are going to be late, do please telephone to avoid people wasting their time.

At many of the smaller companies, there may well be no-one who speaks English. Those places where English is spoken are indicated. Otherwise, go armed with French, or a good phrase-book.

On the other hand, a number of firms are included that are used to receiving tourists and employ multi-lingual guides to look after the visitor. Here the welcome is likely to be less personal and to have a more commercial aspect.

The French *vigneron* is one of the most hospitable men in the world but both his time and his stock are precious. Most growers are happy to offer you wine to taste free of charge, particularly if they think that you might buy some. Others charge for tasting and, again, this is mentioned in the reference column. Often, tasting charges are reimbursed with a purchase.

To spit or not to spit?

This is not an easy question to answer and there are regional variations. In Burgundy, one is generally expected to spit, while in Alsace one is not. If there is a spittoon provided, make use of it; otherwise spit on the floor – if you are in a cellar!

Generally, if more than one wine is offered for tasting, the quality will improve with each wine. Therefore most growers will be flattered if, with the last wine, you say that it is so good that you will not spit it out, but will drink it.

Two things to remember about tasting: firstly a number of wines on an empty stomach can have a noticeable effect, so it is wise to take some ballast on board first. Secondly, drinking and driving is as serious an offence in France as elsewhere and your car can be impounded.

Tasting wine with a grower in the Loire Valley. The tulip-shaped glasses are designed to concentrate the bouquet. Only a limited amount of wine is put in so that it can be swirled about easily, which also helps liberate the flavour, for the greater pleasure of the taster.

CALVADOS

Whilst there is nothing in the way of vineyards around the A13 motorway which leads from the Channel ports of Caen, Le Havre and Dieppe to Paris, there are the apple orchards of Normandy, which produce the only non-grape spirit of France to have its own *appellation contrôlée*: Calvados.

Like the finest vineyard regions, the area is split into a number of smaller areas, each producing its own style of spirit. In all there are some eleven different regional appellations of Calvados, but the finest comes from the Pays d'Auge, which lies on both sides of the river Touques – which flows into the English Channel at Deauville. The centre of the region is Pont l'Evêque. The Pays d'Auge Calvados is distilled from cider in exactly the same way as Cognac is made from wine. There is a double distillation in copper 'pot' stills. The resultant spirit, which is approximately 70 per cent pure alcohol, has a distinct roughness, which is smoothed out by many years' ageing in oak casks. The strength is then reduced before bottling and sale.

A number of the cellars and distilleries are open to the public and for those with rather more time on their hands, there is the *Route du Cidre* circuit. This is best joined by taking the D49 south from the Cabourg exit on the A13, or at Cambremer, which is off the D50, west of Lisieux. Farms on the circuit have a Cru de Cambremer sign.

CALVADOS
Christian Drouin et Cie. Distillerie des Fiefs Ste Anne, Gonneville-sur-Honfleur, 14600 Honfleur. Tues-Sat 0800–1200, 1400–1800.TF.WS.E. Calvados, cider, perry.
S.A. des Calvados Boulard Distillerie du Moulin de la Foulonnerie, 14 Coquainvilliers. Tel:31 62 29 26. Every day 1 Apr-15 Sep, 16 Sep-30 Mar, Mon-Fri.TF.WS.E. Audio-visual show.

MUSEUM
Musée du Calvados et des Métiers Anciens, Pont l'Evêque (on the road to Deauville). Every day. Free entrance.

FOR FURTHER INFORMATION
B.N.I.C.E. 30 rue de l'Oratoire, 14300 Caen.

To buy or not to buy?

Are you expected to buy some wine at the end of the visit? No way are you obliged to, but no grower can make a living by pouring limitless numbers of free glasses of wine. Certainly, there is less obligation if you have paid for your tasting.

If you do buy wine, you will pay French V.A.T. of 17.6 per cent. One way of avoiding this, if you are buying cases of wine, is to buy it with an *acquit* (receipt). You are then given a document that you have to present to the customs both on leaving France and on arriving in your own country. Some growers are unhappy to sell wine in this way as they have to pay the tax if the customer does not see the customs!

Do you tip the person who shows you round? Certainly not if it is a family affair, but with a large company the palm of the guide might, at the end of the visit, be seen to hover. A small token would be appreciated.

Here's to many happy tastings.

Champagne

Of all the wine regions of France, Champagne is for many people the most readily accessible. Its centre, the ancient city of Reims, is an easy ninety minutes' drive along the motorway from Paris, and, for motorists from Britain, under three hours from the Channel ports.

For centuries, the still, red wines of Champagne used to dispute with Burgundy the title of producing France's greatest wines and learned professors at the Sorbonne University in Paris would write papers on their rival merits.

Whilst Champagne is now famous for its sparkling wines – indeed the word is accepted as a synonym for sparkling wine in many countries, including the United States and Australia – it was not until the beginning of the 18th century that the bubbling wine that we know today was first made in the region. Now, whatever there is to celebrate, one calls for Champagne.

Visitors to the house of Pommery at Reims (see page 18) complete their tour of the cellars near this vast barrel, magnificently carved by Gallé.

The vineyards

On the map, the main vineyards of Champagne take the form of a double hook, with the shank lying along the valley of the river Marne. Here is the town of Epernay, where many of the great Champagne companies are based.

To the north, sweeping back in a loop, are the vineyards of the Montagne de Reims, with above them the town of Reims itself, its massive cathedral dominating the rolling countryside. Most of the other important names of Champagne have their cellars here.

The southern barb of the hook is known as the Côte des Blancs. There are also two other areas where Champagne is produced. To the north of Reims lies la Petite Montagne: many miles to the south-east are the remnants of what used to be the important vineyard area of the Aube. There is now a renaissance of Champagne production here, but also a specialised rosé wine, Les Riceys, made from the Pinot Noir grape.

Though Champagne is for the most part a white wine, it is made largely from a blend of red and white grapes. The red grapes come mainly from the valley of the Marne and the Montagne de Reims; the white from the Côte des Blancs.

The skill in creating one of the great wines of Champagne lies in taking wines from a number of sources and styles, and putting them together to make a glorious whole.

To get to Champagne
Reims is 142km (88miles) E of Paris on the A4; 282 km (176miles) S of Calais by the N43, A26 and N44 from Laon.

Champagne vineyard area

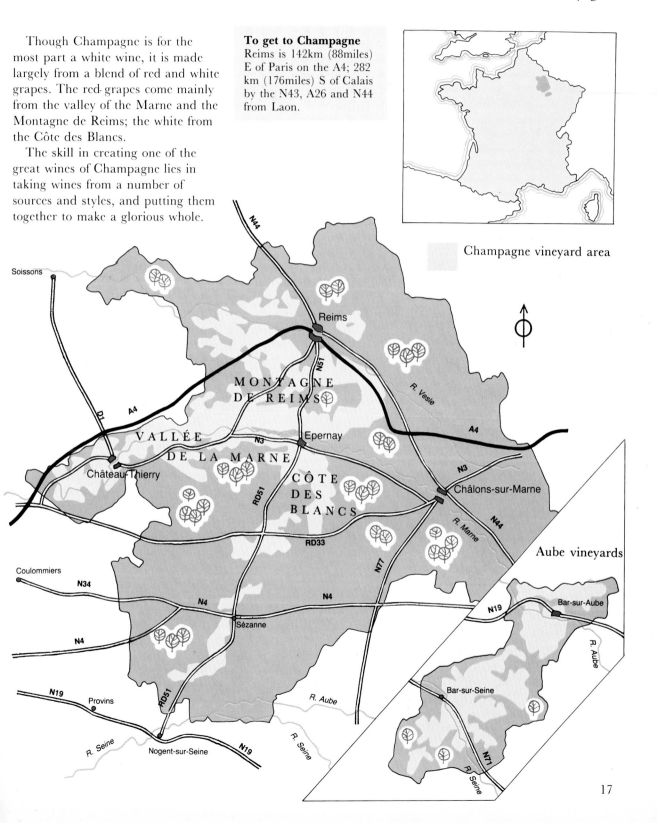

17

Reims

REIMS
Champagne Pommery & Greno 5 place du Général Gouraud, 51100 Reims. Tel:26 05 05 01. Mon-Fri 0900–1100,1400–1700, Sat-Sun (and holidays) 1000–1100, 1430–1630. WS.E. The cellars cover 18km (11 miles).
Champagne Ruinart 4 rue des Crayères, 51100 Reims. Tel:26 85 40 29. (Public Relations Department) By appointment only Mon-Fri 0900–1130, 1430–1600. TF.WS.E. Gallo-Roman cellars, a national historic monument.

An historic city

In some ways, the greatest moments of Reims seem to have been in the past. There still remains one of the four triumphal gates to the Roman city, the Porta Martis, which was reputedly built by Agrippa in honour of the Emperor Augustus.

For more than six centuries, the Kings of France were crowned in its Cathedral, and it was here in 1429 that Joan of Arc begged the newly crowned King Charles VII to be allowed to return to tend her flock of sheep at Domrémy.

More recently, Reims has stood in the way of a succession of invading armies from the east. In 1814, it was occupied by the Russians for twenty-four hours, before Napoleon came to recapture it in one of his last successful military operations.

In 1870, for a time it was the headquarters of the Prussian army on its way to capture Paris, and it suffered heavily from bombardment during World War I. The surrender document of the German forces was signed at what is now 12 rue Franklin Roosevelt, on 7 May 1945, to end World War II.

Reims is now an important regional centre, though being challenged as the capital of the Champagne trade by Epernay, and having lost out to Châlons-sur-Marne as the administrative centre of the *département*. It still plays an important role in the textile trade and is a major shopping centre.

From whichever direction you approach the town, it is the Cathedral that stands out. It has been described as the most perfect Gothic church building in the world. It was begun in 1212, and if the original design had been completed it would now have seven towers and spires. Nevertheless, it is still an imposing building and restoration has been sympathetically carried out.

There is some magnificent stained glass including a beautiful rose window and another designed by

A sign at Hautvillers, the village where Dom Perignon did so much to revolutionize the production of Champagne. The traditional bonnet protects the grape-picker from the sun.

Marc Chagall. The façade of the building used to feature six hundred monumental statues, but many of these were dislodged during World War I, and some can now be seen in the nearby Musée Palais du Tau.

Almost as impressive as the Cathedral is the Romanesque St-Rémy basilica, where Saint Remigius, who brought Christianity to the Franks, is buried. Parts of it predate the Cathedral by almost 200 years.

The cellars

Murray's *Handbook for travellers in France*, dated 1884, states: 'The wine merchants very civilly allow strangers to see their cellars and the process of filling and bottling the wine.' Nothing has changed since those days, and many of the major companies are well equipped to receive visitors.

Whilst the cellars of the Reims merchants may be smaller than those of some of their competitors in Epernay, there are some that have one particular distinction: they date back to Roman times.

Murray once again gives an accurate description: 'They...consist of the old chalk pits from which the Romans quarried building materials. They were formed by sinking a well in the rock, enlarging it as they descended, until the circular pit assumed the shape of a bottle, 80 to 90 ft deep and about 60 ft in diameter. By connecting together 4 or 5 such pits by tunnels, and carrying a broad stair down to the bottom, a cellar is made capable of holding 4 or 5,000,000 bottles of Champagne, fitted for the purpose by the cool and equable temperature preserved at all seasons.'

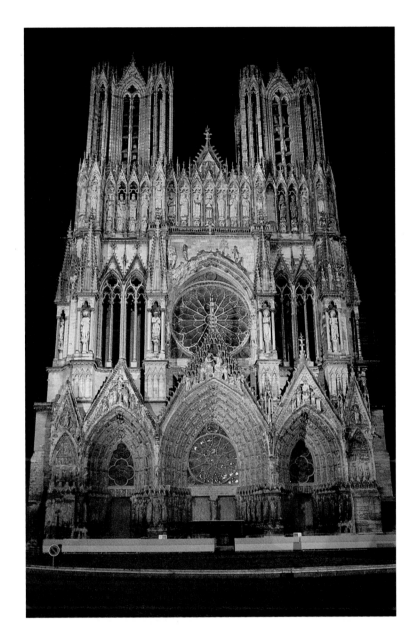

Just as in other vineyard regions, techniques are also changing in Champagne: oak casks are giving way to stainless steel, and the crown cork has replaced the cork stopper during the first fermentation. It is a relief to find that there is still a role for such historical relics as these Roman chalk pits.

A night-time view of the magnificent façade of the cathedral at Reims, where the Kings of France were traditionally crowned. The Gothic building dates back to the 13th century.

Champagne – the Manufacturing Process

The high reputation, and the price, of Champagne are due to a number of factors.

First of all, the vineyards are among the most northerly in the world and, as a result, it is not easy to make wine every year.

Secondly, because red grapes are largely used for making a white wine and a delicate wine at that, particular care has to be taken at the time of picking and pressing. Alone among the major vineyard regions of France, Champagne insists on the grapes being pressed as near to the vineyards as possible, rather than at the winery. Each village will have one or more press-houses.

Pressing

The pressing, too, is tightly controlled, with the grapes being pressed up to five times. The finest wines are made from the first two or three light, rapid pressings. This is known as the *cuvée*. From every four tonnes of grapes, there comes the equivalent of thirteen casks of juice. Ten of these are *cuvée*.

The second, a harder pressing, gives two casks of *première taille* juice, with the final cask coming from the *deuxième taille*.

Fermentation

The juice, or 'must', from all the different villages is then brought to the cellars of the merchant for the first fermentation. When this has taken place, all the distinct wines will be blended together to produce a wine typical of the particular marque.

Bottling

The wine is then bottled, with a little sugar and wine-yeast added for the second fermentation to take place and give the sparkle to the wine. This fermentation leaves a deposit in the wine, and one of the most traditional and time-consuming stages in production takes place to prepare the bottle so that the deposit can be removed without the wine suffering. The object is to disturb the sediment gently and gradually tip the bottle so that it is standing

The cellars of De Castellane Champagne at Epernay. The bottles are resting sur pointe *(upside down) with the deposit in the neck of the bottles.*

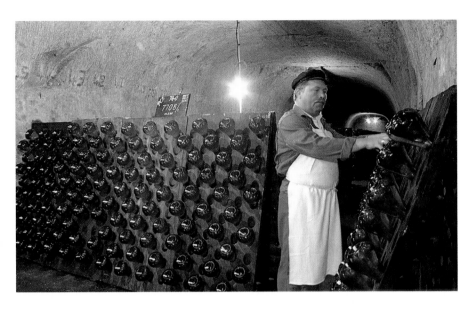

In the cellars of Champagne De Venoge, the remueur *twists the bottles to settle the deposit.*

vertically with the neck downwards and the deposit on the cork.

The traditional way of achieving this was to put the bottles in sloping racks called *pupitres*. Every day, a specialist workman, known as a *remueur*, would give each bottle a quick twist and leave it in a slightly more vertical position. This process involved considerable labour and took several weeks. Now most companies have computer-programmed machines which achieve the same effect in a matter of days, though they keep a token number of *pupitres* for the tourists.

When the deposit has finally settled on the cork, the neck of the bottle is frozen, the cork is removed and the pressure in the bottle forces out the pellet of ice with the sediment in it. The bottle is then topped up with wine and a syrup of old wine and cane sugar, the proportion of which varies according to the degree of sweetness required in the final product. The bottle is recorked, labelled and packed, ready for dispatch.

Because of the enormous pressures involved, the bottles and the corks have to be of the finest quality.

Ageing and blending

Another contributing factor to the price paid by the customer is that most bottles of Champagne remain in the cellars for at least three years before being sold.

Most Champagnes are made from a blend of wines from the different parts of the region and from a number of different years. This enables each company to maintain continuity in style for their wines.

In the best years, however, a company might make a 'vintage' wine, with a date on the label. The controls on the making of such a wine are even more strict.

Is a vintage Champagne better than a non-vintage Champagne? Not necessarily, for the ideal blend for a non-vintage wine should produce an ideally balanced wine, with the weaknesses of the wines of one year being offset by the strengths of those of another.

STYLES OF CHAMPAGNE
Apart from simple vintage and non-vintage wines, there are a number of different styles of Champagne available. Becoming increasingly fashionable is Rosé Champagne. Generally this is made by blending red and white wines before bottling. A Blanc de Blancs wine is one made exceptionally from white grapes alone. Most of the Champagne houses also produce a de luxe *cuvée*, which generally has its own particular styled bottle.

The still wines of Champagne are called *Coteaux Champenois* wine.

The Montagne de Reims and the Marne Valley

AY-CHAMPAGNE
**Champagne Bollinger
S.A.** 9 bvd du Mal. de
Lattre de Tassigny, 51160
Ay-Champagne.Tel:26 55
21 31. By appointment
only. Closed Aug. WS.E.

EPERNAY
**Champagne Möet et
Chandon** 20 ave de
Champagne, 51200
Epernay. Tel:26 54 71 11.
(M. Blanchard) All year,
Mon-Fri 0930–1230,1430–
1730, plus (1 Apr-30 Oct
only) Sat 0930–1200, 1400–
1730, and Sun (and
holidays) 0930–1200, 1400–
1630. TF.WS.E.

MERFY
**Champagne Chartogne-
Taillet** 37–39 Grande Rue,
51220 Merfy. Tel:26 03 10
17. (Elisabeth Chartogne)
Mon-Sat 0800–1900.
Closed during vintage.
TP.WS.E. Picnic area.
Small family company.

Each vineyard village of Champagne
has its own classification, based on
a percentage system, and it is on the
basis of this rating that the grower
is paid for his grapes. At vintage time,
a price per kilo of grapes is fixed and
the grower who has vineyards in a
village rated 100 per cent will receive
the full price. The grower in a village
rated 77 per cent, the minimum
rating, will receive that proportion of
the price.

The Montagne de Reims

In all, there are twelve villages with
the *grand cru* status of 100 per cent
and a further forty-one *premier crus*,
rated more than 90 per cent. Of the
twelve top villages, no fewer than
eight of them come from the most
northerly of the vineyard groupings,
the Montagne de Reims.

   This lies to the south of the city of
Reims, though there are some
vineyards to the north-west around
the village of Merfy. Surprisingly,

many of the best vineyards face north
– generally speaking, the best
exposure to the sun is south-east.
Here the dominant grape is the Pinot
Noir which also produces the great
red wines of Burgundy.

   To join the road which winds
through the wine villages of the
Montagne de Reims, take the RD380
south-west out of the city in the
direction of Château-Thierry. After
8km (5 miles), turn left on to the
D26. This follows the vines round the
foot of the hill all the way to the
beginning of the Vallée de la Marne
vineyards near Bouzy.

The Petite Montagne

The first villages belong to what is
called la Petite Montagne, and it is
not until you have crossed the main
N51 road that you come to the 100
per cent villages of Mailly and
Verzenay, with its well-restored
windmill. Below the road on the left

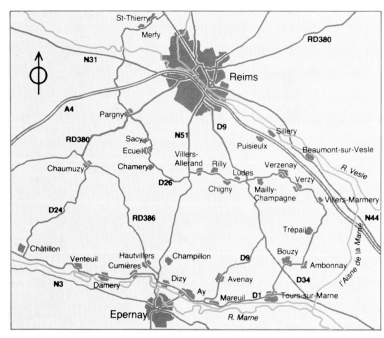

Far left: Looking across the vineyards of the Marne Valley to the village of Hautvillers. In the middle distance are vineyards which have recently been replanted. It will be three years before they can produce Champagne.

Left: Hautvillers, the 'Cradle of Champagne'. Cumières was renowned for its red wines, and in historical times Fismes was notorious for producing 'artificial' colouring wines.

TOURS-SUR-MARNE Champagne Veuve Laurent-Perrier & Co. ave de Champagne, 51150 Tours-sur-Marne. Tel:26 58 91 22. (Mme Borgemeister) Mon-Fri 0900–1030, 1330–1500. Closed Aug. TF.WS.E.

lies Sillery whose wines were for long the most popular Champagnes in England. Beyond Verzenay, the direction the vineyards face changes, first towards the east and then south, where they slope down towards the river Marne. Among the great villages here is Bouzy, noted for its still, red Côteaux Champenois wine.

One of the finest views in Champagne is that of the Marne Valley from the road that leads directly from Reims to Epernay. To the right is Hautvillers, with its abbey, where Dom Perignon experimented so successfully with the wines of Champagne.

Epernay

South of the Montagne de Reims is Epernay, a rather crowded, dull town, with, as its great redeeming feature, the magnificent Avenue de Champagne, flanked by some of the greatest names in the wine trade: De

Venoge and Perrier-Jouet, Mercier and Moët et Chandon.

Some of the cellars are well worth visiting. While these may not be as old as some of those of Reims, they too are cut out of the chalk, and two are so vast that they have to be visited by electric train.

The Côte des Blancs

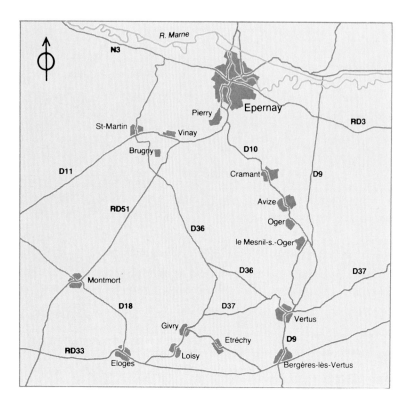

South from Epernay runs the Côte des Blancs, with the vineyards lying on easterly facing slopes below wooded hillsides. Here the other great grape of Burgundy, the Chardonnay, is grown.

The wine made from this grape adds a certain crisp delicacy to the ultimate blend, and it is not surprising in this age when lighter wines are so much appreciated that Blanc de Blancs Champagne is becoming more popular.

The road for visiting these vineyards is the D10 which branches off the main road to the south of Epernay 3 km (2 miles) from the centre of town. The two best-known village names are Cramant and Avize. The first of these is particularly known for its Crémant de Cramant, a wine with a much less aggressive sparkle than that usually associated with Champagne. For some reason, the civil servants in Brussels have decided that the term Crémant will no longer be permitted for Champagne – so this wine's days under that name appear numbered.

The vineyards of the Côte des Blancs finish just beyond the village of Vertus, where there is a most impressive church, with a spring beneath it. Just 5 km (3 miles) further south, a good view back over the vineyards can be had from the top of Mont Saint Aimé, where there are the ruins of an old château.

Southern Champagne vineyards
Although the heart of the Champagne vineyards could be said to finish here, there are three substantial enclaves of vines to the south with every right to the name Champagne. Much of the wine disappears into the blends of the big brands of Reims and Epernay and it is only recently that some of the local growers have begun to make efforts to sell their wines under their own labels.

These vineyards are historical relics of the territories of the Count of Champagne, and indeed at their southern extremity they approach the northern limits of the vineyards of Burgundy.

Of the three vineyard areas, the first, the Côte de Sézanne, is still in the Marne *département* and is effectively a continuation of the Côte des Blancs. The other two areas are in the *département* of the Aube and for many years had to label their wines in a pejorative way as *Champagne Deuxième Zone*. They are Bar-sur-Aube and Bar-sur-Seine. Just outside the former are the remains of

The Côte des Blancs stretching south from Epernay where only the Chardonnay is grown. This grape is used to make Blanc de Blancs Champagne, where no red grapes are used.

LES RICEYS
Champagne Alexandre Bonnet 10340 Les Riceys. Tel:25 29 30 93. (René Bonnet) Mon-Fri 0800–1200, 1400–1800. TF.WS.E. Champagne, Coteaux Champenois red, Rosé des Riceys.

URVILLE
Champagne Drappier 10200 Urville. Tel:25 26 40 15. (Michel Drappier) Mon-Sat 0800–1200, 1400–1800. TF.WS.E. Cellars dating from the 12th century.

FOR FURTHER INFORMATION
C.I.V.C. B.P.135, 51204 Epernay Cedex. Tel:26 54 47 20.

what used to be a Roman camp on the summit of the Colline Sainte-Germaine. This site had two great advantages: not only was it easily defended, but it was well watered by a spring.

Apart from their sparkling wines, the vineyards of Bar-sur-Seine are noted for a still wine with its own appellation, Les Riceys. This is most often a rosé, but occasionally a red wine made from the Pinot Noir grape, and comes much closer to the wine of Burgundy than anything else that one might find in Champagne.

The wine roads in the main part of the Champagne vineyards are well signposted and there are separate routes for the Montagne de Reims, the Vallée de la Marne and the Côte des Blancs.

Alsace

FOR FURTHER INFORMATION
C.I.V.A. Maison du Vin d'Alsace, 12 ave de la Foire aux Vins, 68003 Colmar. Tel:89 41 06 21.

Wine museum
Château de Kientzheim, Kientzheim, 68240 Kaysersberg.

Wine festivals
The festival season starts on 1 May and ends in late Oct; the peak period is July and Aug. In all, there are approximately 45 festivals each year. The main one is the regional wine fair at Colmar, 1st fortnight in Aug. A full list is available from C.I.V.A. address above.

Through the centuries, Alsace has been the bone over which France and Germany have fought. It is only since the end of the First World War that it has been definitively French; indeed some of the older men fought in the German army. As a result the area has a happy blend of styles, in the architecture, in the food and in the wine. However the growers that you will meet are proud that they are neither French nor German: they are *Alsacien*.

With the Vosges mountains as a backdrop the vineyards of Alsace are among the prettiest in France, and those villages that have not suffered in the succession of Franco-German wars are picture-postcard material. Strasbourg and Colmar are two beautiful towns with imposing buildings and museums. Of all the vineyard regions of France, Alsace is, in many ways, the most satisfying to visit.

The dominant feature on any Alsace wine label is likely to be not the name of a village or a vineyard, but rather a grape variety. Here wines are normally made from one of seven different grapes.

Each of these seven has its own characteristics. Only one, the Pinot Noir, gives a red, or more often a deep, refreshing, fruity rosé wine.

Two of the white grapes, the Sylvaner and the Pinot Blanc (or Clevner), give wines for everyday drinking. The Sylvaner, found more in the Bas-Rhin, the northerly end of the vineyards, gives a rather full, earthy wine, while the Pinot Blanc makes a lighter, crisp style, and is often used in making the local sparkling wine, the Crémant d'Alsace.

The four noble grapes
The four noble grapes are the Pinot Gris, known also as the Tokay d'Alsace, the Gewürztraminer, the Muscat and the Riesling. The Pinot Gris is full, soft and supple, often high in alcohol.

The Muscat and the Gewürztraminer both give very full-flavoured wine. The Muscat comes from the same grape as many of the great sweet dessert wines of the world. This

The spire of the Cathedral at Strasbourg, which was completed in 1439. It towers some 143 metres (469 feet) above the historic heart of the cité.

has a similar taste, but is dry. The Gewürztraminer's spicy flavour reminds me of Ogen melons.

Alsace growers are proudest of their Rieslings. At their best, these are classic, steely, austere wines, whose flavour seems to remain in your mouth for ever.

All these wines are dry, but, in the greatest years, sweeter wines are sometimes made from late-picked grapes. The label will then say *Vendange Tardive*, or for the very finest and most expensive wines, *Sélection de Grains Nobles*. These last rate with the finest Sauternes.

Bas-Rhin

Haut-Rhin

To get to Alsace
Colmar is 444km (277 miles) E of Paris – by N4 to Luneville, then N59 and N415; 557km (348 miles) by A4 motorway to Strasbourg then N83; 697km (435 miles) from Calais via Reims; 290km (181 miles) by A36 from Beaune.

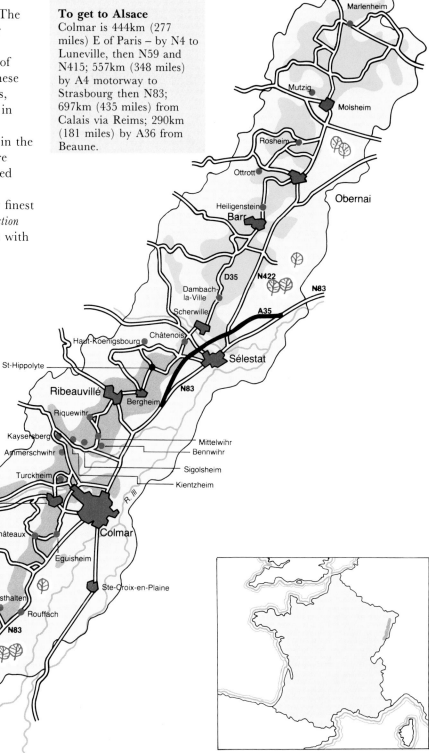

The Bas-Rhin

The Château of Haut-Koenigsbourg, which despite its appearance was built at the beginning of this century by Kaiser Wilhelm II, when Alsace formed part of Germany.

Although the main Alsace wine-road starts at Marlenheim to the west of Strasbourg, there is a small enclave of vines near Wissembourg, some 60 km (38 miles) to the north.

There is an interesting contrast between the host of vines on the German side of the frontier and the few on the French, where all the grapes are sent to the pretty little Co-operative Cellar at Cleebourg.

On the drive up to Wissembourg, the pottery villages of Soufflenheim and Betschdorf, the Forest of Haguenau and such charming half-timbered farming villages as Oberseebach and Niederseebach are worth a visit.

Strasbourg

While Strasbourg itself is away from the vineyard area, the wine-lover can justify a visit there for its numerous *weinstuben*, or wine taverns. These play an important part in the daily life of Alsace and are ideal places in which to taste a range of wines by the glass or bottle and to eat the local gastronomic specialities at a reasonable price.

For the architecturally minded, the cathedral and the old quarter of the city have to be visited.

To reach the wine road from Strasbourg, take the main N4 road west and, after 20km (12.5 miles), you come to Marlenheim. It is here that the main vineyards of Alsace begin. The vinous reputation of Marlenheim is based on its red, or more properly rosé, wine. From Marlenheim, the Route des Vins is clearly marked, as it meanders its way south. For the first few miles, names will strike a chord probably more with beer drinkers than with wine drinkers as one drives through the village of Mützig and passes the modern Kronenbourg brewery.

Villages of the Bas-Rhin

Rosheim still has fortified gateways dating back to the 14th century. If only to get a good view of the vineyards and the plain of the Bas-Rhin, visit the Mont Sainte Odile, above Obernai. Here are the remains of an abbey and a convent to the memory of this 7th-century saint.

Obernai is an attractive town with a beautiful market-place and 16th-century well. Between Obernai and the next town, Barr, comes a succession of pretty villages tucked into the feet of the Vosges mountains. Of these, I can recommend Ottrott as a local base. Heiligenstein even has its own grape variety, the Klevner de Heiligenstein, a type of Gewürztraminer.

Barr is a centre for the tanning industry as well as of the wine-trade. It has an important wine fair each July and is particularly proud of its Gewürztraminer wines.

Just to the south, comes Mittelbergheim, where the best Sylvaners are made and Dambach, which has more vineyards than any other village in Alsace. If you look at the arms of the village, you will see that the dominant feature is a bear. The story has it that a young child once strayed away from the village and came across a wild bear eating mouthfuls of berries. The child was so amazed that he took some home to his parents – and thus the merits of grapes were discovered.

At the southern extremity of the Bas-Rhin *département*, on a crest of the Vosges, is the remarkable Château du Haut-Koenigsbourg. The ideal location for any Dracula film, this castle was built by Kaiser William II, at the beginning of this century, on the ruins of a Swiss feudal stronghold. The winding road up to it gives some sensational views. Just to the north, there is an interesting excursion up the valley of the Giessen. This is the centre for the distillation of the white spirits for which Alsace is noted. Many of the distillers welcome visitors.

Traditional Alsace architecture in the town of Barr. The word winstub *means a bar serving local wines by the bottle or glass.*

The Haut-Rhin

AMMERSCHWIHR
Domaine Sick-Dreyer 17
rte de Kientzheim, 68770
Ammerschwihr. Tel:89 47
11 31. (M. or Mme Pierre
Dreyer) Mon-Sat
0800–1200,1330–1800.
Closed Sun (and holidays).
TF (with purchase of wine)
WS.

BEBLENHEIM
**Cave Vinicole
Beblenheim** 14 rue de
Hoen, 68980 Beblenheim.
Tel:89 47 90 02 (Mme
Anne-Laure Morat) Every
day 0800–1200,1400–1730.
TP. WS.E.

BENNWIHR
**Cave Co-operative de
Bennwihr** 68630 Bennwihr.
Tel:89 47 90 27. (Mme
Steib or Mme Rentz)
Every day 0800–1200,
1400–1800. Closed
Christmas. TP.WS.E.
Restaurant.

There is no great difference in the
scenery between the Haut-Rhin and
the Bas-Rhin, but for the wine-lover
there is a world of difference in the
quality of the wines. With a few
notable exceptions, all the great
wines of Alsace come from the
southern end of the vineyards.

Ribeauvillé
The first wine village in the Haut-
Rhin is Saint-Hyppolite, which, like
Marlenheim is known for its red

*The colourful façade of a house at Riquewihr, one
of France's most beautiful wine-villages. Many
cellars here are open for wine tasting.*

wines, but the first of the great
villages is Ribeauvillé. Perhaps the
finest Riesling of Alsace, the Clos
Saint Hune, comes from here and, to
balance it out, there is an important
bottling plant for mineral water.

The last Sunday in August is
known here as the *Pfifferday*, or
Piper's Day. Each year there are
colourful festivities, with free wine
flowing in the Town Hall Square.

Riquewihr
Just 4km (2.5 miles) to the south
comes Riquewihr, which must be
one of the most beautiful wine
villages in the world. In an area
which has suffered regularly from the
ravages of war, somehow Riquewihr
has managed to escape, and it
remains to this day a 16th-century
fortified village.

The best time to visit must be in
October during the vintage, for
many of the cellars of both growers
and merchants are on the main
street, the rue du Général de Gaulle.
To refresh yourself, some of the
growers have *weinstuben*, where the
traditional way of taking the new
wine is with walnuts and fresh bread.

As an alternative diversion, there
is also a museum of postal history.

If Riquewihr has escaped damage
in succeeding wars, the same cannot
be said for the neighbouring twin
villages of Mittelwihr and Bennwihr.
They were the scene of some of the
fiercest fighting during World War
II, and were almost totally destroyed.
They have now been rebuilt in
traditional Alsace style.

The Weiss Valley
Shortly after these two villages, the
Route des Vins turns off to the right
up the valley of the Weiss. The first

A girl in traditional costume poses in Kaysersberg, where Albert Schweitzer was born. Here, many of the houses date back 500 years.

village, Sigolsheim, was also destroyed in World War II, but Kientzheim still has a fortified gateway, with a sculpture of a man's head putting out his tongue at any assailant, and a château, which is the base of the Confrerie Saint-Etienne, the local drinking brotherhood. Here they hold their regular banquets and maintain a wine museum.

To the left of the road between Kientzheim and the next village, Kaysersberg, lies the Weinbach, a wine estate that used to belong to a Capuchin convent.

Kaysersberg

Kaysersberg's history goes back to Roman times, when it guarded the end of a pass leading out on to the plains of Alsace. Many of the buildings that remain date back to

the 15th and 16th centuries. It is the proud birthplace of Albert Schweitzer.

In Kaysersberg, the wine road again turns back on itself, down the N415, through the important wine village of Ammerschwihr, to the centre of the wine-trade of Alsace, Colmar.

In Ammerschwihr the regional wine fair takes place in August, in the exhibition hall to the north of the town. There is no better occasion on which to taste a full range of wines from throughout the region.

KAYSERSBERG
Paul Blanck et Fils 32 Grand' Rue, Kientzheim, 68240 Kaysersberg. Tel:89 78 23 56. Sun 0900–1200, 1400–1900. TF.WS.E.

RIQUEWIHR
Daniel Wiederhirn 7 rue du Cheval, 68340 Riquewihr. Tel:89 47 92 10. 1100–1200, 1300–1330, 1800–2000. TF (with purchase of wine) WS. Small grower's cellars from 16th century.
Dopff "au Moulin" 68340 Riquewihr. Tel:89 47 92 19. (M. Herold). Every day (in season) 0800–1200, 1400–1800. TP.WS.E. Sparkling wines.
Hugel et Fils S.A. 3 rue de la Première Armée, 68340 Riquewihr. Tel:89 47 92 15. (Etienne Hugel or David Ling) Mon-Thur 0800–1200, 1330–1730 Fri 0800–1200. Closed last week Jul, 1st 2 weeks Aug, and vintage time. TF.WS.E. Very old cellars, including oldest wine cask in use in the world. Tasting shop opens at other hours.
Vins Preiss-Zimmer 42 rue du Général de Gaulle, 68340 Riquewihr. Tel:89 47 92 58. (M. or Mme Zimmer) Every day in season 0900–1200, 1300–1930. Closed 15 Nov-31 Mar. TP.WS.E. 16th-century cellars.

31

Alsace is a region of fine food – here is a display of a local baker's work. On the right are two of the local Kugelhopf cakes.

EGUISHEIM
Vins Wolfberger Cave Vinicole Eguisheim, 6 Grand, Rue, 68420 Eguisheim. Tel:89 41 11 06. (Yves Lithard or Véronique Relly) Every day 1000–1200, 1400–1800. TP.WS.E.

GUEBWILLER
Domaines Schlumberger 100 rue Théodore Deck, 68500 Guebwiller. Tel:89 74 27 00. Mon-Fri 0800–1200, 1400–1700. Closed 1–15 Aug. TF.WS.E.

HUSSEREN-LES-CHATEAUX
Vins Kuentz-Bas 14 rte du Vin, Husseren-les-Châteaux. Tel:89 49 30 24. (Christian or Jean Michel Bas) Mon-Fri 0900– 1200, 1400–1800 Sat 0900–1200. Closed Sun (and holidays). TF.WS.E.

ROUFFACH
Vignobles Mure, Clos St Landelin, RN83, 68250 Rouffach. Tel:89 49 62 19. Mon-Sat 0800–1700. TF.WS.E.

Colmar

Colmar is an ideal base for visiting the vineyards of Alsace. It is also very beautiful in its own right. Well worth visiting are the old quarter, with its network of canals, and the Musée d'Unterlinden.

A chain of villages

While Colmar may make a convenient break in the Alsace wine road, the hardy traveller will cut across from Ammerschwihr to the walled village of Turckheim, where, every evening in summer, the nightwatchman, with halberd and lantern in hand, walks round telling all the inhabitants to go to bed.

Eguisheim

Eguisheim is another in the chain of beautiful Alsace villages. Its cobbled streets are alight with flowers and even its co-operative cellar, the largest in Alsace, blends into the general picture.

The village's most famous son is Pope Leo IX, who was Supreme Pontiff during the middle of the 11th century.

Above Eguisheim, half-way up the hillside, lies Husseren-les-Châteaux, itself dominated by the ruins of three castles on the Vosges skyline.

Rouffach

The wine villages continue in a chain on the slopes above the fast-moving traffic of the N83. This skirts the pretty village of Rouffach, whose wines were described a quarter of a century ago, as having a 'spiritual' bouquet.

Perhaps surprisingly, one of its vineyards, the Clos St-Landelin, has a micro-climate claimed to be the driest in all of France. St Landelin was an itinerant Irish monk who came to convert the Germans during the 4th century and founded a monastery, just across the Rhine, in the Black Forest.

Guebwiller

Of all the Alsace wine-towns, Guebwiller must be the least attractive. It owes its size, and its wealth, to the textile machinery factories of the Schlumbergers. Since the time of the French Revolution, this family has built up what is now the largest single wine domain in

Alsace – and the largest single hillside wine property in France.

This now extends to 140 hectares (340 acres), spread along south-facing slopes overlooking the town. It is so steep in places that tractors are unable to work the vines and a team of twelve horses is still kept for the purpose (and for a natural supply of manure).

The end of the wine road

Towards its southern end the *Route des Vins* seems to lose its purpose for a while, as the vineyards become fewer and the landscape becomes dominated by the potash mines in the plain. However it comes to a glorious finale with the Rangen vineyard, of volcanic soil, overlooking the town of Thann.

Most of the wine villages of Alsace that the traveller may wish to visit lie in a narrow strip along the flanks of the Vosges, and there is no easy circuit that can be made. Nevertheless, because of their wines, their beauty and their hospitality, even the shortest visit to any part of them is always rewarding.

A land of plenty

Well endowed with agricultural and natural resources, Alsace is rich too in traditional foods. As a local saying has it, 'The Frenchman likes to eat

In the Riquewihr cellars of grower and merchant Hugel is the oldest wine-cask in the world still in use. Called the Sainte Catherine, it was constructed in 1715. (Particulars of the company will be found on page 31.)

well, the German likes to eat a lot, the *Alsacien* likes to eat well – and a lot.'

With fine food and wine at fair prices, Alsace is a happy hunting-ground for the thrifty gastronome.

70 cl

ALSACE
APPELLATION ALSACE CONTRÔLÉE

GEWURZTRAMINER

CHARLES SCHLERET PROP. VITICULT. A TURCKHEIM H! RHIN
MISE D'ORIGINE   FRANCE

WINTZENHEIM
Vins Josmeyer 76 rue Clémenceau, Wintzenheim, 68000 Colmar. Tel:89 27 01 57. (Mme Kempf or M. Jean Meyer) Mon-Fri 0900–1130, 1400–1700, Sat 0900–1130. Closed Sun (and holidays). TF.WS.E.

Burgundy

I f there is one vineyard region in France that has the image of living life to the full, it must be Burgundy. Whether it fully lives up to this rôle is for the visitor to decide, but there is no doubt that it is a land of robust wine and hearty food. For the Burgundian, nouvelle cuisine only exists in fairyland, and not the land of good fairies, at that.

Burgundians are proud of their history; once their Dukes ruled territory that stretched as far as what is now Belgium. They are proud, too, of their wines and it is this pride that makes them happy to show them off and talk about them to every visitor who shows a genuine interest. Burgundy has a reputation not just for its food and wine but also for its hospitality.

The vineyards of Burgundy are spread between four different *départements*, the Yonne, Côte d'Or, Saône et Loire and the Rhône – and between five separate and largely distinct regions: Chablis and the Auxerrois, the Côte d'Or, the Côte Chalonnaise, the Mâconnais and the Beaujolais.

While the reputations of the wines of Burgundy and Bordeaux wines may be on a par, in an average vintage Bordeaux produces two and a half times as much wine.

Another interesting comparison is to consider the total production of Burgundy to be one bottle of wine. Out of that bottle, just one glassful comes from the Yonne and the Côte d'Or – from those vineyards which give the wines that have made the reputation of Burgundy: Chablis and Meursault; Nuits-Saint-Georges and Beaune; Pommard and Gevrey-Chambertin. By far the bulk of the production comes from the vineyards of the Beaujolais and the Mâconnais.

Vintage time in Burgundy. Grape-picking in the Beaujolais with the hill of Brouilly in the background. The tractor is specially designed to drive over the rows of vines.

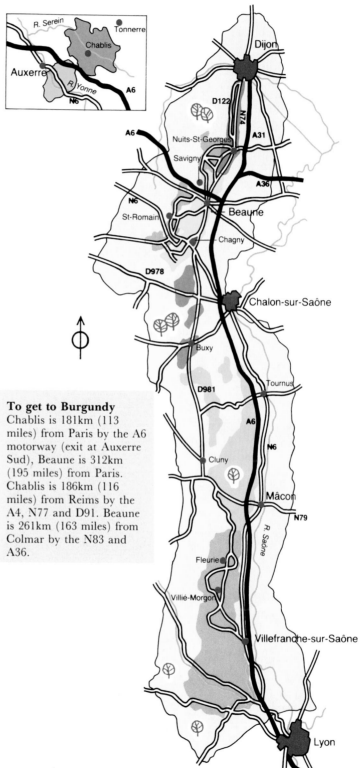

Chablis
Auxerrois
Côte de Nuits
Hautes-Côtes
Côte de Beaune
Côte Chalonnaise
Mâconnais
Beaujolais

It is because of this small production that the great wines of Burgundy are never cheap. It must also be said that eating in Burgundy is not cheap either, particularly if you want a well-known named wine with your meal.

A voyage of discovery

Here, then, is one of the attractions of the region: seeking out the lesser-known wines and the good restaurants off the beaten track. There are fine discoveries to be made in the small villages away from the main roads.

The expansion in the number of hotel rooms in such towns as Beaune and Nuits-Saint-Georges bears witness to their popularity as tourist centres. I would suggest that you see there what has to be seen, but there is much else besides in Burgundy.

To get to Burgundy
Chablis is 181km (113 miles) from Paris by the A6 motorway (exit at Auxerre Sud), Beaune is 312km (195 miles) from Paris. Chablis is 186km (116 miles) from Reims by the A4, N77 and D91. Beaune is 261km (163 miles) from Colmar by the N83 and A36.

Chablis

BEINES
Domaine Alain Geoffroy
4 rue de l'Equerre, Beines,
89800 Chablis. Tel:86 42 43
76. Every day, 0800–1200,
1400–1800. TF.WS.E.

CHABLIS
Domaine Vocore et Fils
40 rte d'Auxerre, 89800
Chablis. Tel:86 42 12 53.
(M. Claude Vocoret)
Mon-Fri 0800–1200,
1330–1730. TP.WS.
La Chablisienne 8 bvd
Pasteur, 89800 Chablis.
Tel:86 42 11 24. Mon-Sat
0800–1200, 1400–1800 (plus
Sun during summer).
TF.WS.E.

The grand cru *vineyards of
Chablis all lie on one hillside
behind the town. These vines are
at Vaudésir.*

When you first see the small town of
Chablis, there is a certain feeling of
anti-climax. It seems surprising that
such a little place should have
become synonymous throughout the
world with dry white wine. While
there may still be vast quantities of
so-called Chablis produced in
California and Chablisse may be a
top seller in New Zealand, the real
thing comes from just here, and a few
surrounding villages.

Renaissance of Chablis
Historically, the reputation of
Chablis was based on
communications, for the wines could
simply be shipped downstream to
the ever-thirsty market of Paris.
However, the soil is poor and the
climate severe, so when the added
burden of the phylloxera plague

arrived at the end of the last century,
many of the vineyards were simply
abandoned and allowed to return to
scrub. It is only during the past
twenty years or so, when increased
demand and improved techniques
have made replanting profitable, that
the true renaissance in Chablis has
occurred.

Classification
There is a rigid hierarchy in the
classification of the wines of Chablis.
At the top come the seven *grand cru*
vineyards, and these lie together on
one slope just a few hundred metres
to the north-west of the town, across
the river Serein.

From left to right, as you face, the
hillside, they are Bougros, Les
Preuses, Vaudésir, Grenouilles,
Valmur, Les Clos (the largest and
my favourite) and Blanchots.

Next there come a host of *premiers
crus*. These lie on southerly facing
slopes on both sides of the river and
of the small valleys that run off it.
Perhaps the best-known *premier cru*
wines are Montée de Tonnerre,
Fourchaume, Vaillons and
Montsmains.

Ordinary Chablis comes from a
number of small surrounding
villages, where the stony soil is a
limestone based on shells from
before the time of man.

Finally comes Petit Chablis, made
in declining quantities in villages on
the fringe of the area.

Recent changes
As replanting has taken place the
area under vines and the total crop
have increased considerably over the
recent past, more than ten times in
the past forty years and four times in
the last twenty.

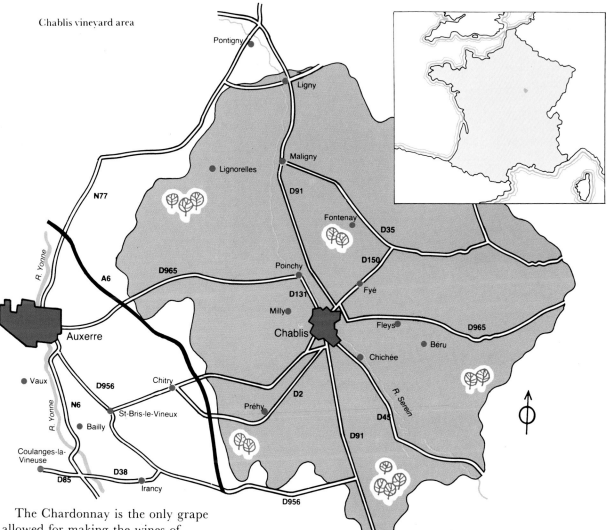

Chablis vineyard area

The Chardonnay is the only grape allowed for making the wines of Chablis, and it gives a steely, dry wine that is the ideal match for shellfish.

Over the past few years, the style of the wines of Chablis has gently altered, perhaps as a result of the demands of the market. True austerity seems to be something of the past. Nowadays a degree of softness is often present.

The town of Chablis
Despite the fact that during the last war it suffered as a result of an extempore air raid from the Italian air force, much of old Chablis survives. There are a number of houses dating back to the 14th and 15th centuries, and the Porte Nöel, which was rebuilt in 1770.

At the end of a series of narrow streets, the door of the parish church, begun in the 13th century, is covered with horseshoes. These are offerings to Saint Martin, the patron saint of horsemen and all things equestrian.

FOR FURTHER INFORMATION
C.I.B. rue Henri Dunant, 21200 Beaune.
Tel:80 22 21 35.

Wine festival
Chablis Wine Fair, last Sat and Sun of Nov.

The Yonne

A traditional grower's cellar in the village of Irancy, noted for its full-blooded red wines. Here, the cellars are deep underneath the houses on both sides of the main street.

Former glories

Historically, the Yonne Valley was the part of Burgundy with the greatest number of vineyards. A combination of the extreme climate, phylloxera, the coming of the railway (enabling wines to be brought to Paris cheaply from the vineyards of the south of France) as well as the increasing availability of other forms of employment, led to their being almost totally abandoned, apart from a hard core at Chablis.

Now, there is a renaissance in the wines of the Yonne, and not just in the wines of Chablis. While there are about 2,000 hectares (4,800 acres) of Chablis vineyards, there are a further 1,000 hectares of vineyards producing a variety of other wines.

Crémant de Bourgogne

Perhaps the most exciting development has taken place in a former quarry and in the mushroom cellars in the village of Bailly on the banks of the river Yonne, just off the N6, south of Auxerre. Here, in 1972, 80 growers banded together to form a company to produce sparkling Crémant de Bourgogne. With a stock of some four million bottles and an average of two thousand visitors a week this has now become a very large scale operation.

A local speciality

Up a steep, narrow road behind Bailly lies the mother village of Saint-Bris-le-Vineux, which is by far the most important vineyard village in the Yonne *département*, outside the Chablis vineyards. The streets are full of growers' houses, with beneath them narrow, deep cellars. Many of the growers make wines from the Chardonnay and Aligoté grapes, but there is also a local speciality, the Sauvignon de Saint-Bris. This is the only place in Burgundy where this grape is grown, and it gives a wine that is similar in style to Sancerre.

Just 4km (2.5 miles) away is the village of Chitry-le-Fort, renowned for its Bourgogne Aligoté. Here there is a fortified church dating back to the 13th century.

The vineyards of Irancy are intermingled with cherry orchards and they produce a full-bodied red wine from the Pinot Noir and the César, a traditional local grape. The soil is very similar to that of Chablis, and oyster fossils can be picked up everywhere. The vines are in a natural amphitheatre, which is a sun-trap. The vineyard with the highest reputation is la Palote. On the west bank of the river Yonne lie two vineyard villages, Coulanges-la-Vineuse and Vaux. At Coulanges a softer red wine is made from the Pinot Noir and at Vaux there is the charmingly named vineyard of Dessus-Bon-Boire, which, loosely translated, means 'above good drinking'!

Auxerre

The most important town in the region is Auxerre, which has a very pretty old quarter and the Gothic cathedral of Saint Stephen. There is also a 15th-century clock tower, with not only a sundial but also a moondial.

Of the formerly famous vineyards of Auxerre, there is only one survivor, the Clos de la Chaînette, which is run by the local psychiatric hospital and which produces agreeable Bourgogne blanc and rosé.

It is worth mentioning two historic vineyards that have recently been reconstituted. The first is the south-facing Côte Saint Jacques, which overlooks the town of Joigny. Here most of the wine made is a *vin gris*, or pale rosé, from the Pinot Noir and Pinot Gris.

Finally, visitors to the splendid church built to honour the remains of St-Mary-Magdalene at Vézelay can now taste the local wine for the first time this century, for some of the local growers have joined together to plant some 20 hectares (50 acres) of vines to make both red and white wine.

Looking down on the village of Irancy from the vineyards. As well as producing wine, the village has a high reputation for its cherries. Many of the local people own both orchards and vines.

IRANCY
Robert Colinot Irancy, 89290 Champs sur Yonne. Tel:86 42 20 76. (Mme Rosa Colinot) By appointment only. TF (if you purchase wine). WS.

ST-BRIS-LE-VINEUX
Domaine Luc Sorin 13 bis rue de Paris, 89530 St-Bris-le-Vineux. Tel:86 53 36 87. (M. or Mme Sorin) Mon-Sat 0900–1200, 1400–1900. Closed Sun (and holidays) TF (if you purchase 12 bottles). WS.
Sicava, Caves de Bailly 89530 St-Bris-le-Vineux. Tel:86 53 34 00. (M. Alain Corenlissens or M. Claude Cardot) 3 Apr-28 Sep, Wed and Sun, at 1530. Otherwise Mon-Fri 0800–1200, 1400–1800, by written appointment only. TP (free glass and tasting of sparkling wines and liqueurs). WS.E. Visit and tasting last approximately 1 hour.

FOR FURTHER INFORMATION
C.I.B. rue Henri Dunant, 21200 Beaune. Tel:80 22 21 35.

Wine museum
89580 Coulanges-la-Vineuse.

Wine festivals
Festival of St Vincent, Sun nearest 22 Jan, Coulanges-la-Vineuse. Sauvignon Festival, 2nd weekend in Nov, St-Bris-le-Vineux.

Sancerre and Pouilly-sur-Loire

While it may seem strange to include the vineyards of Sancerre and Pouilly-sur-Loire in the section on Burgundy, there is some logic in it, for Pouilly lies administratively within the region of Burgundy and the main vineyards of the Loire are twice as far away as those of Chablis.

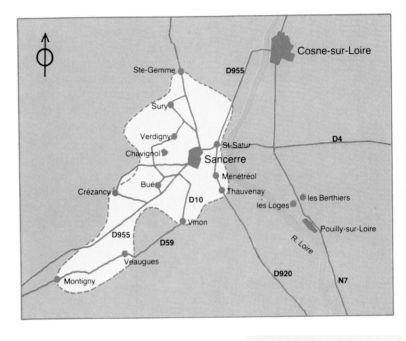

Sancerre – the town

The town of Sancerre lies on a hill dominating the left bank of the River Loire. Its strategic importance has long been recognized, and some believe that it is the Cortona of Caesar's *Commentaries*. The château now belongs to the Marnier-Lapostolle family, major local vineyard owners, one of whose ancestors created the Grand Marnier liqueur.

Sancerre – the wines

Sancerre is known mainly for its white wine made from the Sauvignon grape. It is perhaps in Sancerre that the Sauvignon best shows its characteristics, with a green stalkiness that you either love or hate. However an increasing quantity of red and rosé wine is now being made from the Pinot Noir.

The wines are produced in Sancerre itself and 13 other surrounding villages. As far as reputation is concerned, perhaps the most important is Bué. Here the best-known vineyard is the Chêne

SANCERRE
Caves de la Mignonne
Tel:48 54 07 06.
Gitton Père et Fils
Chemin de Lavaud,
Menetréol sous Sancerre,
18300 Sancerre. Tel:48 54
38 84. (M. Pascal Gitton)
Every day 0900–1200,
1400–1900 (Sun by
appointment only). Closed
Christmas. TF.WS.E.
Domaine wines from
Sancerre and Pouilly.

FOR FURTHER
INFORMATION
L'Union Viticole
Sancerroise, 16 bis, ave
Nationale, 18300 Sancerre.
Tel:48 54 03 51.

Wine museum
Musée de la Vigne 18300
Verdigny en Sancerre.

The village of Sancerre is dominated by its château. Fine wines are made here from the Sauvignon grape.

Marchand, which gives some of the finest wines. Another famous local vineyard is the Clos de la Poussie. At Bué the Caveau des Vignerons serves light meals as well as the local wines.

A local cheese

The Monts Damnés vineyard is split betwen the two villages of Verdigny and Chavignol. This latter village has also given its name to the second local gastronomic speciality; the goat's milk cheese called Crottin de Chavignol, which is protected by its own *appellation contrôlée*. My French dictionary politely tranlates *crottin* as droppings – the cheese is, after all, small in size! It can be sampled, together with the local wine, in the underground Caves de la Mignonne, which are just north of Sancerre, on the road to Saint-Satur.

Pouilly-sur-Loire

If you take the D4 eastwards out of Sancerre, as soon as you have crossed the River Loire, you are in the vineyards of Pouilly. Here, two grapes are grown, the Sauvignon and the Chasselas.

Of these two, the Sauvignon makes the classic wine, the Pouilly Blanc Fumé, which is a similar wine to Sancerre though lacking some of its aggression. The Chasselas, on the other hand, is something of an historical anomaly. It was originally grown as a table grape for the Parisian market, but has remained to make an agreeable uncomplicated wine labelled as Pouilly-sur-Loire.

The largest producer of Pouilly Blanc Fumé is probably Patrick de Ladoucette, who owns the Château de Nozet, just north of the town of Pouilly. As well as making wine from

The Château de Nozet, where Patrick de Ladoucette makes much of the finest wine of Pouilly-Fumé. The château dates back to the middle of the last century.

his own vineyards he buys both juice and wine from other growers. The finest wines from his own vines, he sells under a luxury presentation with the name of Baron de L.

Another attractive property, producing full-bodied wines is the Château de Tracy, on the right of the road from Sancerre.

Two hamlets whose names often appear on wine labels are Les Loges and Les Berthiers, on either side of the N7 trunk road, which now by-passes the town of Pouilly. At Les Loges, the vineyards rise steeply above the Loire. Because it is a natural sun-trap, it produces perhaps the most full-bodied wines in the area.

Among the major vineyard owners of Les Berthiers is the Domaine Saint-Michel, which also has vineyards in Burgundy, and which has behind it the Côte d'Or merchants Prosper Maufoux.

Prominent among the local growers are a number of members of the Daguenau family.

POUILLY-SUR-LOIRE
Domaine Guy Saget RN7, 58150 Pouilly-sur-Loire. Tel:86 39 16 37. (M. Jean-Louis Saget) Mon-Fri 0800–1200, 1400–1800 Sat, Sun 1000–1800. Closed Christmas and New Year's Day. TF (with purchase of wine) WS.
Guy Baudin Les Loges, 58150 Pouilly-sur-Loire. Tel:86 39 02 54. From 0830 each day. Closed Sun evenings. TF.WS.

FOR FURTHER INFORMATION
Syndicat Viticole de Pouilly, Les Loges, 58150 Pouilly-sur-Loire. Tel:86 39 12 65.

Wine Festival
Second weekend in Aug.

The Côte d'Or

When one thinks of the wines of Burgundy, the first to come to mind are probably those of the Côte d'Or. While they only represent a small proportion of the total production, they include most of the great names.

No one knows for certain when the vines were first planted. There is evidence that the local inhabitants enjoyed wine as long ago as 500 BC, for the difficult part of the tin road – from Cornwall to the eastern Mediterranean – lay between the headwaters of the River Seine and its tributaries and the valley of the River Saône. Here the Aedui, predecessors of the Burgundians, acted as porters – and they took wine as a significant part of their pay.

In about 400 BC, a vast number of the Aedui crossed the Alps and settled in northern Italy. The main reason for this was, according to Plutarch, that 'They found this drink so delicious that, on the spot, they prepared their arms and crossed the Alps, with their wives and children, in search of the country that produced such a wine.'

It is probable that when they returned to Burgundy, a century and a half later, they brought vines and a knowledge of wine-making with them. It is certain that, during the Roman occupation, many wine estates were established in what are the better-known vineyard villages.

The wine of prince and prelate
With Burgundy's importance as an independent kingdom, and then as a semi-autonomous duchy, the reputation of its wines spread far and wide. Their fame, too, was helped by the fact that for more than six hundred years all the most famous vineyards belonged to either the nobility or the church. Thus the wines were drunk in all the most

Summer work; trimming the vines to help the sun get to the grapes, taking place here in le Montrachet, the finest of the white Burgundy vineyards

important royal and ecclesiastical circles in Europe.

Dijon

Dijon, the administrative and commercial capital of Burgundy, now has comparatively little to do with the wine trade. Industrial expansion has left little of the vineyards that it used to boast. However, it still has a high gastronomic reputation for its liqueurs, particularly the crème de cassis de Dijon, a controlled appellation, its gingerbread and its mustards. These and many other products are on show at the Dijon Gastronomic Fair, which takes place each year in early November.

The town centre is still full of old streets, most of them just a short walk from the tourist office in the Place Darcy.

The cathedral of Saint-Bénigne is the fourth church on the site and dates from the end of the 13th century. Originally a Benedictine abbey, what used to be the monks' dormitory is now an archaeological museum.

Other churches that should be visited include Notre-Dame, Saint-Jean and Saint-Michel.

The former Palace of the Dukes of Burgundy now houses the Town Hall and what is supposed to be the best art gallery in France outside Paris.

To get to the Côte d'Or
From Chablis by the D91, A6 and A38, Dijon is 135km (85 miles) and by the D91 and A6, Beaune is 130km (81 miles).

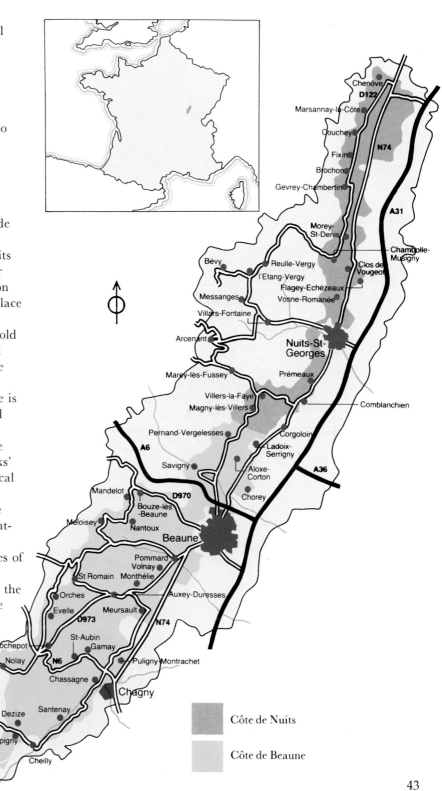

Côte de Nuits

Côte de Beaune

The Côte de Nuits

The remains of the château of Gevrey-Chambertin, most of which was destroyed in the 16th century.

GEVREY-CHAMBERTIN
Domaine du Clos de Tart
Morey-Saint-Denis, 21220 Gevrey-Chambertin. Tel:80 34 30 91. (M. Perraut) Mon-Fri 0900–1100,1400–1700. Closed mid-Sep to mid-Oct. WS. Two levels of cellars dug out of the rock. 16th-century wine-press.

FIXIN
Domaine P. Gelin 2 rue du Chapitre, Fixin, 21220 Gevrey-Chambertin. Tel:80 52 45 24. Mon-Fri 0900–1200,1400–1800. TF (with purchase) WS.

COUCHEY
Derey Frères 1 rue Jules-Ferry, Couchey, 21160 Marsannay la Côte. Tel:80 52 15 04. (M. Maurice Derey) Mon-Fri 0800–1200, 1400–1700. TF.WS.

MARSANNAY-LA-COTE
Domaine Fougeray de Beauclair 44 and 89 rue de Mazy, 21160 Marsannay-la-Côte. Tel:80 52 21 12. Every day 0900–1900. TF.WS.E.

VOUGEOT
Château de la Tour Clos de Vougeot, 21640 Vougeot. Tel:80 62 86 13. (M. or Mme Labet) Every day 1000–1900. Closed end Nov-1 Apr. TF (with purchase) WS.E. Typical vaulted cellars within Clos de Vougeot itself. Largest owners of vines in Clos de Vougeot.

A choice of routes

Driving south from Dijon along the Côte d'Or, the motorist has a choice of three roads. If you are in a hurry, take the A31 motorway and then, to visit the vineyards, take the exit either at Nuits-Saint-Georges or at Beaune. Alternatively, take the N74 main road, which has lesser vineyards on either side, or D122, the Route des Grands Crus, which slowly wanders through the famous wine villages of Burgundy.

Chenôve

To join the Route des Grands Crus, take the N74 and after some 5km (3 miles), at Chenôve, turn right at the L'Escargotière restaurant.

The vineyards of Chenôve have suffered greatly from the expansion of the city of Dijon and there are now only a quarter of the growers that there were 25 years ago. The most important feature in the village is the former press-house of the Dukes of Burgundy, with two enormous wine-presses dating back to 1238.

The first vineyard village of importance is Marsannay-la-Côte, which has traditionally been known for the best rosé wines in Burgundy. It has recently been granted its own village appellation for white and red wines, so there is a real danger that the rosé wines may slowly disappear. The next village, Couchey, also has the right to sell its wines under the name of Marsannay.

Fixin may be said to be the first village on the Côte to produce great red wines, with the Clos de la Perrière probably being the outstanding vineyard.

A souvenir of Napoleon

For Imperialists, the village is a living memory to the Emperor Napoleon, thanks to an adopted son of the village, Claude Noisot. He shared Napoleon's exile at Elba and fought at the battle of Waterloo. In later life, Napoleon became his fixation. He renamed a local vineyard Clos Napoléon and created a park in his memory, with, eventually, a museum, a florid statue of the Emperor rising to lead the world again, and his own tomb, where he was buried, standing on guard.

Gevrey-Chambertin

After Brochon comes Gevrey-Chambertin, perhaps the capital of the red wines of Burgundy. Driving along on the southern side of the village, the vineyards read like a roll-call of honour: Mazis-Chambertin, Ruchottes-Chambertin, Clos de Bèze, le Chambertin and Latricières-Chambertin.

On looking at the soil there is little to show that where the sign reads *Ici commence le Chambertin*, real greatness begins.

Morey

Like many of the villages of Burgundy, Morey has tacked on to its name that of its most famous vineyard, the Clos Saint Denis, and has become Morey-Saint-Denis. Its other greatest vineyards are the Clos de la Roche, the Clos de Tart and the Clos des Lambrays.

Chambolle-Musigny

The vineyard of Bonnes-Mares is shared by Morey with its neighbour Chambolle-Musigny. Here the finest wines come from le Musigny, which makes a minute quantity of white wine each year, in addition to an outstanding red. In the centre of the village is a magnificent lime tree, planted on the instructions of Sully, Henri IV's minister.

Clos de Vougeot

Down the slope from the vineyard of le Musigny is the Clos de Vougeot, a walled vineyard founded in the 12th century by the monks of Cîteaux. Within the *clos* of 50 hectares (120 acres), there are almost eighty owners, each making his own wine. The Château, which now belongs to the Confrérie des Chevaliers du Tastevin, was originally built as the press-house and cellars for the monks.

Château du Clos de Vougeot Every day, Apr-Oct 0900–1900 Oct-Apr 0900–1130, 1400–1730. Collection of old wine implements. Press-house, with four old presses.

Wine festival
Carrefour de Dionysos, Ist Fri in Apr, Morey-St-Denis.

The Clos de Vougeot, the largest vineyard on the Côte d'Or. The château was once the centre of the wine domaine of the Cistercian order of monks. Now it is the headquarters of the local drinking brotherhood, the Confrérie des Chevaliers du Tastevin.

NUITS-ST-GEORGES
Ets. Moillard 2 rue Fr. Mignotte, 21701 Nuits St Georges. Tel:80 61 03 34. Mon–Fri 0900–1100, 1500–1700. Closed Aug. TF.WS.E.

VOSNE-ROMANEE
Domaine Lamarche rue de la Fontaine, 21700 Vosne-Romanée. Tel:80 61 07 94. (M. or Mme Lamarche) Mon–Fri 0900–1200, 1400– 1700. Closed 2nd half of Aug and 1st week in Sep. TF (with purchase). WS (minimum 4 bottles per wine). E.

Rion Père et Fils
Rte Nationale, 21700 Vosne-Romanée. Tel:80 61 05 31. (M. Bernard Rion) By appointment only. TF (with purchase). WS.E. M. Rion also breeds Bearded Collies and Berger de Brie dogs, and is happy to show them to visitors.

Wine festival
Sale of wines from the Hospices de Nuits, 1st Sun in Apr.

After Vougeot, the next vineyards belong to the village of Flagey-Echézeaux. As the village lies to the east of the main road and is undistinguished, its claim to fame must be its two grands crus les Echézeaux and les Grands Echézeaux. Its lesser wines can be sold under the name of the next, and infinitely more famous, village of Vosne-Romanée.

Vosne-Romanée
In the crown of the red wines of Burgundy, this must be the diamond in the centre. Its wines have gained a justified reputation for their unrivalled finesse and bouquet. While some would claim that the Romanée-Conti is the finest, there are others who would vote for La Tâche. Close behind come such other great wines as La Romanée, Romanée-Saint-Vivant, Richebourg and La Grande Rue.

Romanée-Conti and La Tâche belong exclusively to the Domaine de la Romanée-Conti, La Romanée to the Liger-Belair family, and La Grande Rue to the Lamarche domain. In the circumstances, each bottle is allocated carefully – and at a price.

Once again, there is little to distinguish these noble plots of earth. To visit them, you go up the narrow lane by the side of the church. On the slope in front of you, a simple cross marks Romanée-Conti.

Nuits-Saint-Georges
Because the main road skirts the fringes of Nuits-Saint-Georges, few

The most expensive agricultural land in the world, the vineyard of Romanée-Conti, with the village of Vosne-Romanée beneath it. At the beginning of the century, many Burgundian villages added to their name that of their most famous vineyard. Thus Vosne became Vosne-Romanée.

visit the town itself. Besides its host of merchants' cellars (Nuits comes second only to Beaune in importance in the Burgundy wine trade) there is the beautiful 13th-century church of St Symphorien.

Though it has been much destroyed in a succession of wars, the town still maintains a bustling air of history. The fame of its wines owes a great deal to the prescriptions of the royal physician Fagon, who cured Louis XIV of a fistula by liberally dosing him with Nuits. In honour of this, the main street is now named after him.

The importance of the town and its wines have led to this northern part of the Côte d'Or vineyards being called the Côte de Nuits.

Prémeaux

South of Nuits, the next village is Prémeaux, within whose boundaries are produced many of the finest *premier cru* wines of Nuits-Saint-Georges.

Prémeaux also has a number of natural springs, and until 1970 the water from one of them was marketed commercially. Its medical properties were recognized in Roman times.

Comblanchien and Corgoloin

The Côte de Nuits finishes with the two villages of Comblanchien and Corgoloin. Sadly, neither has been able to establish an individual reputation for its wines and they are sold simply as Côte de Nuits Villages.

Comblanchien is perhaps better known now for its marble, which was widely used in the construction of the Paris Opéra and Orly airport.

The name of the last vineyard on the Côte de Nuits, the Clos de

The domaine of the vineyard of Clos de Tart at Morey-Saint-Denis, now the property of Mâcon wine merchants Mommessin. It takes its name from its mediaeval owners, the nuns of Tart-le-Bas.

Langres, is a reminder of the past importance of the church in the viticultural history of Burgundy. It used to be the property of the Bishop and Chapter of Langres, a town to the north of Dijon, who, until the French Revolution, were the largest vineyard owners in Burgundy, after the Cistercian order of monks.

Red Wines of the Côte de Beaune

While the Route des Grands Crus on the Côte de Nuits is easy to follow, for the villages are arrayed in a straight line, on the Côte de Beaune there are more twists and turns and often there can be a choice of roads.

Ladoix-Serrigny is the first of the villages that one comes to; the reputation of wines under its own name comes below those that it makes on its higher slopes, which can be sold under the *grand cru* names of Corton Charlemagne for white wines and, with rare exceptions, Corton for red. (One exception is the Cuvée Paul Chanson belonging to the Hospices de Beaune, which is a white wine coming from Corton-Vergennes.)

To the left of the main road, as you come out of the village there is an 11th-century chapel, probably built for pilgrims on their way to Santiago de Compostella.

Aloxe-Corton

Aloxe-Corton, as well as its *grand cru* vineyards, boasts the colourfully roofed Château Corton-André built at the end of the last century and the more sober Château Corton-Grancey, belonging to wine company Louis Latour. Behind it, carved out of a quarry, are perhaps the finest cellars in Burgundy, with the estate press-house above.

The third of the villages producing Corton and Corton-Charlemagne is Pernand-Vergelesses. Tucked into a narrow valley in the hillside, it is perhaps the least spoilt of all the wine villages of the Côte d'Or, with some beautiful growers' houses.

Savigny and Chorey-lès-Beaune

Savigny lies at the mouth of the valley of the Fontaine Froide and is particularly known for its red wines. In the valley lies an imposing château, which was rebuilt at the beginning of the 18th century.

On the plain, beyond the N74, is the village of Chorey-lès-Beaune where a number of important estates are based. The church has a belfry in the 'foreign' style of Franche-Comté and there is a picturesque château surrounded by a moat.

Pommard

The first vineyard village after Beaune is Pommard, famous throughout the world for its full-bodied red wines. The main street winds off to the right from the D973, with growers' houses on both sides. The village has three châteaux, two of which have now been united as the Château de Pommard and belong

The village of Aloxe-Corton. Its two neighbouring villages can also use its name for their wines.

Vintage time in Burgundy. Emptying the plastic crates of freshly-picked grapes into the trailer for them to be taken back into the press-house.

to the Laplanche family. The oldest is the Château de la Commaraine belonging to the Jaboulet-Vercherre family and backing on to the attractive Clos de la Commaraine vineyard.

Volnay

As another village standing back from and above the main road, Volnay maintains an agreeable calm, with its finest vineyards lying out on the slope in front of it.

In historical times, the Dukes of Burgundy spent the summers in the château that they built here, though unfortunately its destruction was ordered by Cardinal Richelieu.

Monthélie

To find the village of Monthélie, you must turn right off the main road on to the D23. It is a village of narrow streets and wine growers' houses spread down the hillside and with a

reputation of poverty, because there are no sources of water on its territory. Being slightly off the main road, its wines have not the quality image that they so rightly deserve.

CHOREY-LES-BEAUNE
Domaine Germain
Château de Chorey-lès-Beaune, 21200 Beaune. Tel: 80 22 06 05. (François or Marie-Pierre Germain) Mon-Sat 0900–1200, 1400–1800. Closed Aug. TF.WS.E. Attractive château, rebuilt in 1668.

POMMARD
Château de Pommard
21630 Pommard. Tel: 80 22 07 99. Every day 0830–1830. Closed 3rd Sun in Nov–26 Mar. TP.WS.E. Beautiful cellars and buildings.

SAVIGNY-LES-BEAUNE
Domaine P. Dubreuil-Fontaine Père et Fils
Pernand-Vergelesses, 21420 Savigny-lès-Beaune. Tel: 80 21 51 67. Mon-Fri 0900–1200, 1400–1830 Sat 0900–1200. Closed Sat afternoon, Sun, holidays, 1–25 Aug. TF.WS.

49

The Town of Beaune

Beaune must be one of the most satisfying wine towns to visit because of its compactness. It is still circled by its town walls, built in the 13th and 14th centuries, and, while the town has now expanded far beyond this military corset, most that is of interest lies within. The origins of the town go back to Roman days and on a town plan the circular trace of the oppidum can still be seen.

In these days of peace, the walls and towers of the fortifications are used to store wine, and while expanding business and modern machinery have led many companies to construct new premises outside the town, most of the important ones still have their offices and much of their stock in the town centre.

While Bouchard Père et Fils, Chanson Père et Fils and Calvet store their wine in the bastions with walls up to 7 metres (22 feet) thick, other companies, such as Patriarche and Ponnelle, use dispossessed religious properties. Drouhin have the former cellars of the Dukes of Burgundy.

The Hôtel-Dieu

Among the architectural gems of the town, the most famous must be the Hôtel-Dieu, built in 1443 by Nicolas Rolin, Chancellor of the Duchy of Burgundy, as a 'hospital for the accommodation and assistance of the poor and the sick'. Built in the Flemish style, with high, colourful roofs, around a beautiful courtyard, its treasures include a polyptych of the Last Judgment by Roger van der Weyden.

The Hôtel-Dieu forms part of the Hospices de Beaune (the other part is the Hospice de la Charité in the rue de Lorraine) financed by

considerable endowments, including an important estate of vineyards, whose wine is auctioned off each year on the third Sunday in November.

In the picturesquely named rue d'Enfer is the former Palace of the Dukes of Burgundy, which now houses an attractively laid out wine museum. Close to this is Notre-Dame, the parish church of Beaune.

Other buildings of interest include the Town Hall in what used to be

the cloister of an Ursuline convent and, beyond the town wall on the road to the north, the simple 13th-century church of St Nicholas.

To the west of the town, on the flanks of the hillsides split by two valleys, lie the vineyards that have made Beaune so rich and spread its name throughout the world. While nearly all the wine that is made is red, the variety of soils and micro-climates give a variety of styles that is matched by the wines of no other commune in Burgundy. There are devotees of the Grèves vineyard, of the Clos des Mouches, of Bressandes and of Fèves; each gives a great wine in its individual style.

Until recent years, there has been a grave shortage of reasonably priced hotel rooms in Beaune. Recent building has solved this problem and it is now a good halt on the motorway for a one-night stay, or longer.

The courtyard of the Hôtel-Dieu at Beaune. This building dates back to the beginning of the 15th century, when the Duchy of Burgundy stretched as far as the Low Countries, which accounts for the architecture, most particularly of the roofs, which are tiled in the Flemish style.

Built as a hospital for old people, it is financed by large endowments, particularly vineyards, made over the centuries.

51

White Wines of the Côte de Beaune

While there are some who might claim that Burgundy does not produce the finest red wines of France, there are few who would say that it does not make the best dry white wines. Here come together the perfect blend of soil, climate and the Chardonnay grape to give great wines with fruit and flavour.

As we have already seen, the village of Aloxe-Corton produces great white wines in the Charlemagne vineyard, but it is the three villages of Meursault, Puligny-Montrachet and Chassagne-Montrachet that bear the reputation for making the best of white wines.

Meursault

Meursault is a useful centre for visiting the vineyards of the Côte d'Or. There are a number of small hotels and restaurants and a camping site, with a swimming-pool.

The village has two châteaux. The older, dating from the 14th century, was largely destroyed in 1478; what remains now forms part of the town hall. The Château de Meursault is built above the 14th-century cellars of the Cistercian monks. Here there is now an art gallery and the chance to taste a range of fine burgundies.

On the main N74 road are the ruins of a leper-house, built in 1180 by Hugues de Bourgogne. The village church is also worth visiting. Its most outstanding feature is its spire, the tallest in the region.

Puligny-Montrachet

Puligny-Montrachet is a much quieter village, with its two squares ringed by imposing private houses. Once again there are two châteaux. The 'old' one was partly dismantled and sold off to antique dealers during World War I. The 'Château de Puligny-Montrachet' dates back to the middle of the 18th century. Its main claim to fame, apart from its wines, appears to be the fact that Laetizia Ramolino, Napoleon's mother, once slept there.

Traditionally, grapes in Burgundy have always been picked by hand, but difficulty in obtaining the necessary labour exactly when it is needed is leading some growers, such as this one in Meursault, to turn to mechanical harvesters.

Through the bars of a gateway in the surrounding wall can be seen the vines of the vineyard of le Montrachet, thought by many to produce the finest white wine in the world.

The great vineyards lie behind the village. Two grands crus, Chevalier-Montrachet and Bienvenues-Bâtard-Montrachet, lie solely within the boundaries; two others, le Montrachet and Bâtard-Montrachet, it shares with its neighbour, Chassagne.

Chassagne-Montrachet is best known for its white wines, but it actually produces rather more red wine, much of it of a very high quality. The village I find to be something of a disappointment.

Santenay

From Chassagne, the vineyard road, the D113A, curves round the hillside to the last of the major vineyard villages, Santenay. Here, mainly red wines are made.

Santenay has medicinal springs. The water is useful in the treatment of such potential local problems as liver malfunctions, diabetes, obesity and gout. Perhaps more importantly, they entitle Santenay to a casino!

So far, we have kept along the straight road through the vineyards. However, there are villages lying off that road in the valleys to the west.

From Meursault, the D17E leads first to Auxey-Duresses, known for its red and white wines. Next comes the attractive village of Saint-Romain, split into two parts, one on a rocky escarpment, the other in the valley below. There are the remains of a château that dates back to at least the 10th century and which used to belong to the Dukes of Burgundy.

Caves in the imposing cliffs that overlook the village sheltered prehistoric man and there is a small museum of local history in the town hall. Also of interest is a cooperage whose casks might just as well be found in California as Burgundy. The N6, which was the main road from Paris to the south until the motorway was built, leads up to the village of Gamay, which gave its name to the grape, and Saint-Aubin, which produces excellent red and white wines. It is in villages like these that real bargains are to be found.

MEURSAULT
Château de Meursault 21190 Meursault. Tel:80 21 22 98. Every day 0930–1130, 1430–1700. Closed Dec-Feb. TP.WS.E. Art gallery, 14th-century cellars.
Domaine Jacques Prieur 21190 Meursault. Tel:80 21 23 85. Mon-Fri. Closed Aug. WS.E.
Ropiteau Frères 13 rue du 11 Novembre, 21190 Meursault. Tel:80 21 24 73. (M. Delavault, M. Balland or M. Fuso) Every day 0900–1900. Closed 15 Nov-15 Mar. TF.WS.E. 16th-century cellars, formerly the property of the Hospices de Beaune.

PULIGNY-MONTRACHET
Domaine Chartron 13 Grande Rue, 21190 Puligny-Montrachet. Tel:80 21 32 85. Mon-Fri 0800–1200, 1330–1730. Closed Aug. TF.WS.E.
Domaine Laroche Château de Puligny-Montrachet, 21190 Puligny-Montrachet. Tel:80 21 38 38. (Anne Laroche) Sat-Sun 0800–1200, 1400–1800. Closed Aug. TP.WS.E.
Domaine Leflaive 21190 Puligny-Montrachet. Tel:80 21 30 13. Mon-Fri 1000–1200, 1600–1800. Closed holidays and Aug. TF.E. Maximum 6 people.

Wine festivals
La Trinquée de Meursault, 2nd Sat in Sep. La Paulée de Meursault, Mon of 3rd weekend in Nov.

The Hautes-Côtes

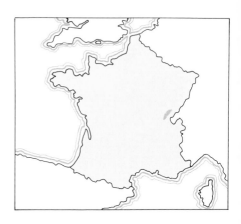

HAUTES-COTES DE BEAUNE
Domaine Mazilly Père et Fils Meloisey, 21190 Meursault. Tel:80 26 01 34 or 80 26 02 00. Every day 0900–1900, by appointment if possible. TF (with purchase) WS.E.
André Guillemard Meloisey, 21190 Meursault. Tel:80 26 01 11. By appointment only. TP.WS. Large range of wines.
J.Joliot et Fils Nantoux, 21900 Meursault. Tel:80 26 01 44. (M. J.B.Joliot) Every day 0800–2000. TF.WS. Picnic area.

HAUTES-COTES-DE-NUITS
Domaine de Montmain Villars-Fontaine, 21700 Nuits-St-Georges. Tel:80 62 31 94. (M. Bernard Hudelol) By appointment only. TP.WS.
Domaine Thévenot-le-Brun et Fils Marey-lès-Fussey, 21700 Nuits-St-Georges. Tel:80 62 91 64. Mon-Sat 0800–1200, 1400–1800. TF.WS.E.

Behind the main vineyards of the Côte d'Or lie others in what are known as the Hautes-Côtes. Here there are not just vines, but also meadows and plantings of soft fruit, particularly blackcurrants, for the crème de cassis liqueur.

Most of the wine that is made is red, though there is also a little white, and much of it is made at the co-operative cellar of the Hautes-Côtes, which is on the N74, on the southern outskirts of Beaune.

The scenery is spectacular. From the top of the cliff at Orches you look down on Saint-Romain, the valley leading down to Meursault, the plain of the Saône, the Jura mountains and, on a very clear day, Mont Blanc.

There is the Château de la Rochepot, nestling in against the hillside; the Pas Saint Martin, near Mandelot, where the saint is reputed to have escaped from the devil by jumping across the valley; the pretty

The Château de la Rochepot was built in the 15th century by Regnier Pot. Almost totally destroyed during the Revolution, it was restored by the French President Sadi Carnot.

town of Nolay, with its 14th-century market hall; and Bévy, with the biggest vineyard area of all, where a local wine-merchant reclaimed land that had been scrub for generations.

This is the quieter, less commercial face of Burgundy, where time seems less important. Many of the growers also own vines in the more fancied villages of the Côte – but their prices always seem more reasonable, because they do not have a fashionable address.

To taste a range of the wines, and simple local food, there is no better place to go than the Maison des Hautes-Côtes, a joint venture of a number of growers at Marey-lès-Fussey on the D8, in the hills above Corgoloin.

At Orches, above Pommard, there are two specialities, a rosé wine and Poire Williams distilled from fruit from the local orchards.

The Hautes-Côtes are visited by too few. They can be seen in half a day – but it is worthwhile taking longer. While the local description of them as the 'Switzerland of Burgundy' seems something of an exaggeration, their quietness, and the variegated landscape, make a relaxing change.

The Jura

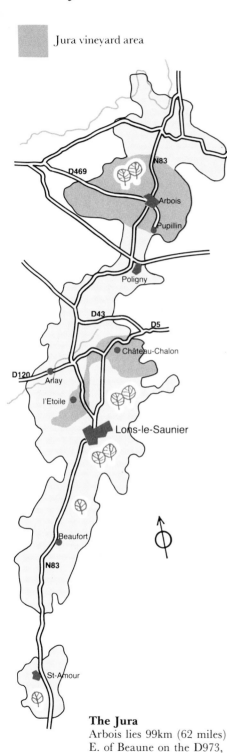

Jura vineyard area

The Jura
Arbois lies 99km (62 miles) E. of Beaune on the D973, N73, N5 and D469.

For what is a comparatively small vineyard area, the Jura produces a remarkably diverse selection of wines. The capital of the region is Arbois, a charming town whose architecture has been influenced by long-past Spanish occupation. It is particularly well known for its rosé wines, reputedly the best in France after Tavel.

More individual is the *vin jaune*, which tastes like a fino sherry and is produced in a similar way. The best of this comes from the small village of Château-Châlon. It is bottled in a traditional bottle called a *clavelin*, containing just 64cl of wine.

Other local specialities are the rich *vin de paille* and the aperitif *macvin*, made like port.

The wines of the Jura are too often forgotten. In some ways they are among the most traditional in France, made in ways and from grapes that are not used elsewhere. The vineyards are worth a visit in their own right, either on the way to Geneva and the ski-resorts, or as an awayday break from the bustle of Burgundy.

ARBOIS
Fruitière Vinicole d'Arbois 2 rue des Fosses, 39600 Arbois. Tel:84 66 11 67. Summer, every day 0900–1230,1400–1830, otherwise by appointment. TF.WS.
Henri Maire S.A. 39600 Arbois. Tel:84 66 12 34. (M. Varigas) Every day 0900–1900. TF.WS.E. Audio-visual presentation, Museum of the Vine and Wine. Birthplace of Pasteur.

BLETTERANS
Château d'Arlay Arlay, 39140 Bletterans. Tel:84 85 04 22. Mon-Fri 0900–1200,1400–1800, weekends by appointment. TF.WS.E. The château can be visited every day in July and Aug.

FOR FURTHER INFORMATION
Société de Viticulture du Jura, ave du 4ème R1 B.P 396, 39016 Lons-le-Saunier.

Henri Maire's tasting-cellar in Arbois.

The Côte Chalonnaise

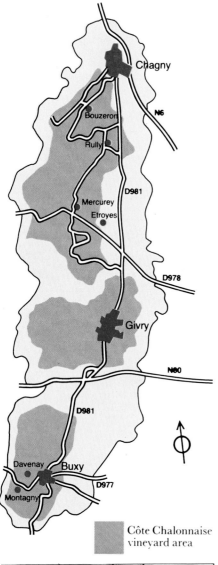

Côte Chalonnaise
vineyard area

For too long the wines of the Côte Chalonnaise have been under-appreciated, but recently there have been two moves to give them more of an individual personality. First, the Aligoté wines from the small village of Bouzeron have been able to call themselves Bourgogne Aligoté Bouzeron – and no other village in Burgundy has been permitted to use its name in this way.

Secondly, up just one level, the red and white wines have been able to add Côte Chalonnaise to their generic name of Bourgogne. This is important, for the wines from the local vineyards, apart from those from the four village appellations of Rully, Mercurey, Givry and Montagny, had too often disappeared anonymously into the blending vats of the large merchants.

Chagny
The starting point for a visit to the vineyards of the Côte Chalonnaise must be the town of Chagny. From there, you take the D981 road to the south, though diversions must regularly be taken to the right to visit the various villages.

Bouzeron
Of these the first is Bouzeron, already mentioned for its Aligotés. The monks of Cluny were the first to establish the reputation of Bouzeron's wines but now Bouchard Père et Fils and Aubert de Villaine, one of the co-owners of the Domaine de la Romanée-Conti, have important holdings here.

Rully
There is a rather steep and narrow road to the next village, Rully, but the faint-hearted may prefer to return

MONTAGNY
Château de Davenay rte de Cluny, 71190 Buxy. Tel:85 92 04 14. (M. Couard) Mon-Sat 0900–1800. TF.WS.

BOUZERON
Chanzy Frères Domaine de l'Hermitage, Bouzeron, 71150 Chagny. Tel:85 87 23 69. (Daniel Chanzy) Mon-Fri 0830–1200,1400–1800. Sat by appointment. Closed Aug. TP.WS.

RULLY
André Delorme rue de la République, Rully, 71150 Chagny. Tel:85 87 10 12. Mon-Sat 0830–1200, 1330–1730. TF.WS.E. Still and sparkling wines from Côte Chalonnaise.
Xavier Noël-Bouton Domaine de la Folie, 71150 Chagny. Tel:85 87 18 59 or 85 87 06 75. Mon-Fri 0900–1300, 1400–1800.TF.WS.E.

MERCUREY
Antonin Rodet 71640 Mercurey. Tel:85 45 22 22. (M. Marc Vachet or Mlle Fabienne Nicot) Mon-Thu 0800–1200,1400–1800 Fri 0800–1200,1400–1700. TF.WS.E. Cellar and vineyard visit, Ch de Chamirey and Ch de Rully.

FOR FURTHER INFORMATION
C.I.B.M. 389 ave Maréchal de Lattre de Tassigny, 71000 Mâcon. Tel:85 38 20 15.

Wine festivals
Concours des Vins de la Côte Chalonnaise et du Couchois, 2nd Sat in Jan. Chagny Wine Fair, about 15 Aug, 4/5 days

to Chagny first. Rully has suffered badly in history and its reputation for its wines has recently improved largely as a result of the efforts of its dynamic mayor, Jean-François Delorme. As well as making fine red and white wines, it is also a centre of the sparkling-wine trade.

Mercurey

The best-known wines of the Côte are Mercurey, and they come from a cluster of small villages of which Mercurey is one. It is known especially for its red wines, which have an equal standing to many from the Côte d'Or.

There are certain 'château' wines with a good reputation. The one most often found is the Château de Chamirey, from local merchants Antonin Rodet.

Givry and Montagny

Givry, too, is well-known for its red wines, though it produces much less than Mercurey. It was a favourite of Henri IV (who always seemed to be prepared to endorse the local wine) and he may well have used it as an aid in his courtship of his local girlfriend, Gabrielle d'Estrées.

The last of the wines of the Côte Chalonnaise is Montagny. This is just white wine from the vineyards around the small town of Buxy, where there is a tasting cellar in the Tour Rouge.

The Château de Chamirey at Mercurey, which belongs to the Marquis de Jouesmnes, Chairman of local wine company Antonin Rodet. The château vineyard produces both red and white wine with the appellation Mercurey.

The Mâconnais

CLESSE
Jean Thévenet Quintaine-Clessé, 71260 Clessé. Tel:85 36 94 03. Mon-Fri, by written appointment only. TP (at taster's discretion) WS.

IGE
Groupement de Producteurs les Vignerons d'Igé 71960 Igé. Tel:85 33 33 56. Mon 1330–1800 Tue-Fri 0730–1200,1330–1800 Sat 0730–1200. TF.WS. Tasting in 11th–century church, collection of old wine implements.

LUGNY
Caveau St-Pierre 71260 Lugny. Tel:85 33 20 27. 1 Mar-1 Nov every day but Wed 0900–2100 2 Nov-25 Dec Sat-Sun 0900–2100. TP.WS.

SERRIERES
Jean-Marc Balendras les Guérins, 71960 Serrières. Tel:85 35 72 94. Every day. Closed 2nd half of Aug. TF.WS. Mâcon red, goat's cheese.

VIRE
Cave de Viré
Envercheron, 71260 Viré. Tel:85 33 12 64. (M. Bené) Mon-Fri 0800–1200, 1400–1800.

All that now remains of the Benedictine Abbey of Cluny, once the most important church building in Europe after St Peter's in Rome.

If you continue along the D981 road that has taken you through the vineyards of the Côte Chalonnaise, you cross the boundary into the vineyards of the Mâconnais at the village of Saint-Gengoux-le-National. The road eventually leads on to the small town of Cluny.

Cluny
Whilst it may not appear to play an important role in the current world of wine, this has not always been the case. Little remains of the great Abbey, which was once the head-quarters of the Benedictine order, and which had been responsible for much of the early vineyard planting in Burgundy.

Cluny is on the western fringes of the vineyard area, which broadly lies in the triangle between Cluny and two towns lying on the river Saône, Tournus and Mâcon.

Saints and churches
Tournus is best known for the magnificent church of St Philibert, where there are the remains not just of that saint but also of St Valerian, who was martyred for his faith in the 2nd century. One thing that gives him a particular, if not peculiar, distinction is that after his head had been cut off, he picked it up and walked away with it. In Tournus there is also a gallery dedicated to the painter Jean-Baptiste Greuze (1725–1805).

For those interested in ecclesiastical architecture, the area is particularly known for its Romanesque churches, largely dating back to the 12th century. Those of Donzy and Blanot are particularly beautiful. Just north of Cluny is the village of Taizé, centre of a worldwide ecumenical youth movement.

The Mâconnais is not solely dedicated to the production of wine. To the west of Mâcon is the town of Charolles, which has given its name to the well-known breed of cattle, the charollais. There are also many herds of goats.

Historically the region was known for its red wines made from the Gamay and Pinot Noir grapes. Now most of the production is in white wine, from the Chardonnay. As this is a region of polyculture, most of the growers take their grapes to the local co-operative cellar, of which there seems to be one in nearly every village. Many of these have tasting cellars for the promotion of their wines to passing tourists.

Mâcon-Villages
Much of the wine from the peripheral vineyards in the area has a right only

to the simple appellation 'Mâcon'. In the heart of the area, though, there are 36 villages which have the right to sell their wine either as Mâcon-Villages, or by attaching the village name to Mâcon, such as Mâcon-Lugny or Mâcon-Viré. Two of the villages have given their names to grape varieties, Chasselas and Chardonnay, while one of them, Milly, has added the name of its most famous son, the poet Lamartine.

To visit the vineyards of the Mâcon-Villages, a simple route would be to leave Tournus by the D56 and drive through Chardonnay and Lugny. From there one takes the D82 and the D85 to Igé and La-Roche-Vineuse. After a brief detour to Milly-Lamartine, where the poet lost a fortune in making wine, you can take the main N79 road into Mâcon.

An alternative, and slightly shorter, route would be from Chardonnay to Uchizy, Viré and Clessé, arriving in Mâcon from the north. Either way gives a pleasant pastoral drive through a gentle, rolling landscape.

Value for money

Now that many of the white wines of Burgundy have become very expensive, it is worthwhile looking at those from the Mâconnais. These are made from the same grape, the Chardonnay, and they bear a family resemblance to their rather more aristocratic cousins from Chablis and the Côte d'Or.

It is in areas such as this that real discoveries are to be made, for, apart from the larger co-operatives, there are a number of smaller growers who are justifiably proud of what they make.

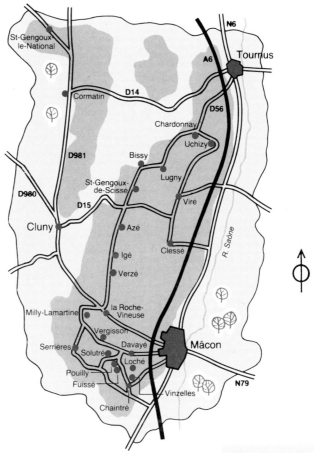

Mâconnais vineyard area

Wine festivals
Concours des Vins de la St Vincent, nearest Sat to 22 Jan, Exhibition Centre, Mâcon.
Haut Mâconnais Wine Fair, Sat before Palm Sun, Lugny.
French National Wine Fair, about 20 May (10 days), Mâcon.

To get to the Mâconnais
Tournus is 53km (33 miles) from Beaune and 364km (266 miles) from Paris by the A6. Mâcon is 83km (52 miles) from Beaune and 395km (247 miles) from Paris.

MACON
Maison Mâconnaise des Vins ave de Lattre de Tassigny, 71000 Mâcon. Tel:85 38 36 70. Every day 0800–2100. TP.WS.E. Light meals.
Société Mommessin La Grange Saint Pierre, 71009 Mâcon. Tel:85 34 47 74. (M. Bardet) Mon-Fri 0900–1200, 1400–1630. Closed between Christmas and New Year. WS.E.

VINZELLES
Cave des Grands Crus Blancs 71145 Vinzelles. Every day 0800–1230, 1400–1930.TP.WS.

FOR FURTHER INFORMATION
C.I.B.M. 389 ave de Lattre de Tassigny, 71000 Mâcon. Tel:85 38 20 15.

The Château de Fuissé where Monsieur Vincent makes outstanding Pouilly-Fuissé, one of the great white wines of Burgundy.

Greatest Wines of the Mâconnais

To the west and south of Mâcon are the vineyards of Pouilly-Fuissé and its satellites, Pouilly-Vinzelles, Pouilly-Loché and Saint-Véran. These are the greatest wines of the Mâconnais and, Pouilly-Fuissé particularly, have created for themselves a worldwide reputation.

Mâcon

They lie on the doorstep of Mâcon, a beautiful town despite the fact that its buildings have suffered badly over the centuries. It is the administrative capital for the region and its wines. It has had a wine fair since the first half of the 14th century and, since 1933, has held the annual French National Wine Fair, where wines from all over France and often further afield can be tasted for a nominal sum.

For the motorist hurrying down the motorway to the beaches of the Mediterranean or the Alpine ski-slopes, Mâcon can make a convenient halt, with its many fine restaurants and hotels. If there is no time to visit the neighbouring vineyards, a full range of the local wines can be tasted, with or without a light meal, at the Maison Mâconnaise des Vins, on the way into the town from the north.

A famous crag

The vineyard skyline of Pouilly-Fuisse is dominated by two dramatic crags, the rocks of Vergisson and Solutre. For some reason that I have never discovered, that of Vergisson appears to have played no role whatsoever in history, while that of Solutré has kept the archaeological diggers busy for more than a century. The main reason for this has been the rather basic way in which the local prehistoric man killed wild horses and, to a lesser extent deer. He simply drove them off the edge of the precipice and then, presumably, went down to pick up the pieces.

Pouilly-Fuissé

The vineyards of Pouilly-Fuissé are in a natural amphitheatre of vines spread between the four villages of Vergisson, Solutré, Fuissé and Chaintré. The wines are all dry and white, though they have a deep richness of body that is not found elsewhere in Burgundy. I do not know whether it is this or the name that appeals to the American

consumer, but, because of the small production and the enormous demand, the wines of Pouilly-Fuissé tend to be expensive.

Fortunately, the adaptability of the Burgundian producers has created a small number of alternative, if lesser, wines from the same region. The production of two of these, Pouilly-Loché and Pouilly-Vinzelles, is quite small, but about 20 years ago, the new appellation of Saint-Véran was created to satisfy some of the demand.

This wine comes from a small number of villages surrounding the vineyards of Pouilly-Fuissé. Some of them formerly made, and still can make, Mâcon-Villages; the others make Beaujolais blanc, for here the vineyards of the Beaujolais and the Mâconnais overlap.

Vineyard circuit

The circuit of these vineyards of the southern Mâconnais is short and simple, though rather windy. Leave Mâcon by the D54 and shortly after passing under the motorway, fork right to Davayé, where there is the local wine school, and Vergisson.

On the far side of the village, you turn left and drive round the back of the rock of Solutré to the village of the same name.

From Solutré, the road leads to Pouilly and the picturesque village of Fuissé, where there is a sign saying, 'A hundred growers bid you welcome.' Some of the best wine comes from the Château de Fuissé. From here there is a narrow lane down to Loché and Vinzelles, but it is probably easier to drive round via Chaintré. Here the choice is either a return to Mâcon or an attack on the Beaujolais.

POUILLY-FUISSÉ

APPELLATION CONTRÔLÉE

Georges Greffet   375 ml

Propriétaire-Récoltant · 71960 Solutré-Pouilly

The vineyards of Pouilly-Fuissé are dominated by the rock of Solutré. In prehistoric times, hunters drove wild horses in their thousands to their death from the summit.

The Beaujolais

FOR FURTHER INFORMATION
U.I.V.B. 210 bvd
Vermorel, 69400
Villefranche-sur-Saône.
Tel:74 65 45 55.

Wine festivals
Fête Raclet Romanèche-Thorins, last Sat Oct.
Various fairs in Fleurie, Juliénas and Brouilly, Nov.
Beaujolais Wine Fair, 1st Dec weekend, Villefranche.

A cellarman in Villié-Morgon studies a glass of the cru *Beaujolais, Morgon. Behind him on the barrel-head is what looks like a watering can. This is used for topping up the wine barrels.*

For many wine lovers, the Beaujolais is the most enjoyable of all wine regions. It has a relaxed atmosphere that is all its own. It is a place where the importance of time seems to be eternally diminished and thus it is the wrong place for those who want to break away from the motorway just to gain a small sample of its flavour.

The flavour of the Beaujolais is not just its wine or its countryside – a succession of rounded hills leading ultimately to the beginnings of the Massif Central. It is the red-roofed villages round the squares where the click of boules is rivalled by the clink of bottle on glass at the tables outside the welcoming bars.

A wine to be enjoyed

Beaujolais, as a wine, does not seek to be taken too seriously. It is there to be enjoyed, and if it is difficult to prove the local claim that Beaujolais

is the only wine that can quench a thirst, there is every incentive to put it to the test by taking another glass . . . and another.

Even with detailed instructions, it is easy to get lost, for the contours do not permit straight roads, and in any case they might speed up the pace of life.

The *Clochemerle* novels of Gabriel Chevalier are not an exaggeration of that life in the Beaujolais, but rather a loving look at it.

Geography of the Beaujolais

Broadly speaking, the Beaujolais can be divided into two parts. In the south, beyond Villefranche-sur-Saône is the Bas-Beaujolais. Here the soil is largely sandy, and lighter, earlier-maturing wines are made; most of those wines that we see as Beaujolais Nouveau.

In the north, between Mâcon and Villefranche, the soil is more granitic. From here come the fuller, fruitier wines of the Beaujolais-Villages and the ten *crus*, those villages that can sell their wine just under their own names.

Throughout the region, the red wines are made with just one grape, the Gamay. This is despised in the rest of Burgundy, but in the Beaujolais it is king.

Alternative routes

The main road, the N6, skirts the eastern fringes of the Beaujolais vineyards. While the villages along it may house many of the most important wine merchants of the region, and while there may be the occasional tasting cellar to cause the hurried motorist to halt for a while, to taste and perhaps to buy, this is not the Beaujolais.

To get to the Beaujolais
Villefranche-sur-Saône is
439km (274 miles) from
Paris and 31km (20 miles)
from Lyon on the A6.

Sixty years ago, two local writers, Léon Foillard and Tony David, suggested a three-day circuit by car in the Beaujolais. The modern alternative is a choice of three different Beaujolais 'routes', which are clearly marked. Two of these lie between Mâcon and Villefranche, whilst the third, *au pays des pierres dorées*, meanders round the southern part of the region.

With the modern motorist in mind there is also a 'fast' route, which turns off the N6 at Crêches-sur-Saône, 8kms (5 miles) south of Mâcon, and leads through the famous *crus* beginning with Saint-Amour, then Juliénas, where there is a beautiful château, largely rebuilt at the beginning of the 18th century, and the earlier arcaded Maison de la Dîme, where church tithes were collected.

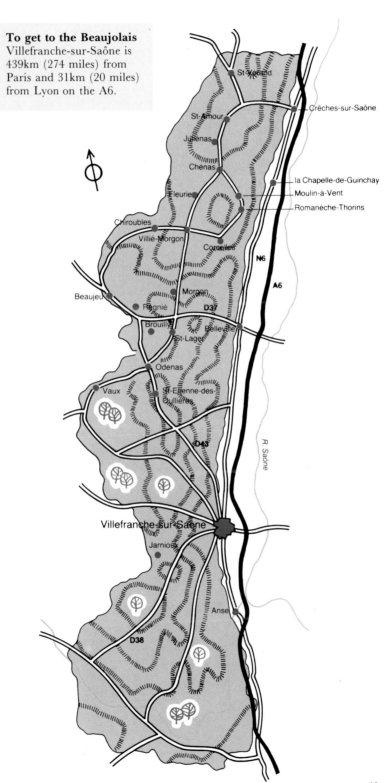

The Chateau de la Chaize at Odenas is one of the most beautiful properties in the Beaujolais. The property's vineyards produce an excellent Brouilly.

BEAUJEU
S.C.I. Pavillon de Chavannes Chavanne, Quincié, 69430 Beaujeu. Tel:74 04 35 01. (Mme Vidal) Mon-Fri 1400–1800. Closed summer holidays. TF.WS.E.

BROUILLY
Mme La Marquise de Roussy de Sales Château de la Chaize, Odenas, 69460 St Etienne-des-Oullières. Tel:74 03 41 05. (Mme Martray) Mon-Fri 0800–1200,1330–1800. Closed Aug, 1 week at Christmas, 1 week at Easter. TP.WS. E.

MORGON
Domaine des Pillets les Pillets, 69910 Villié-Morgon. Tel:74 04 21 60. (M. Brisson) Mon-Sat 0900–1200,1400–1800. Closed 1st 10 days in Aug. TF.WS.E.

MOULIN-A-VENT
Château des Jacques Moulin-à-Vent, 71570 Romanèche-Thorins. Tel:85 35 51 64. Mon-Fri 0930–1200,1400–1700 Sat-Sun by appointment only. TF (with purchase) WS.E. **Château Portier** Moulin-à-Vent, Romanèche-Thorins, 71570 La Chapelle de Guinchay. Tel: 85 35 51 57. (M. Georges Noblet) Mon-Fri 0800–1200,1400–1730. Closed Aug. TF (with purchase) WS. Range of crus and red, rosé and white Beaujolais.

Moulin-à-Vent, Fleurie and Morgon

Within the boundaries of Chénas is the sole windmill of the Beaujolais, but perhaps one of the best known in the world, for it has given its name to the wine Moulin-à-Vent.

From Fleurie the route goes to Villié-Morgon and the hamlet of Morgon, from where it is worthwhile making a short diversion to the left to visit the beautiful Château de Pizay.

Brouilly

Saint-Lager lies at the foot of the Mont de Brouilly, at the top of which is a small chapel, the Nôtre-Dame du Raisin, the object of a well-refreshed pilgrimage each year on 8 September. There is a road to the top, from where there is a magnificent view of the Beaujolais vineyards.

Odenas

At Odenas is the Château de la Chaize, built at the end of the 17th century by the nephew of the confessor of Louis XIV. The gardens were designed by Le Nôtre and the cellar is a national monument, the longest single vaulted cellar in the Beaujolais. From there the rapid route passes through Saint-Etienne-des-Oullières to Villefranche.

The *route touristique*

The *route touristique* follows largely the same outline but with a number of diversions. The first takes in the Château de Corcelles, which is open to the public.

The second is the former capital of the region, Beaujeu, which like Beaune has a hospital financed in part by its vineyard holdings.

The Château also owns La Grange Chartron at Régnié, which was built as an immense vineyard estate building at the beginning of the last century.

Régnié also has the distinction of being the last village to have its wines elevated to *cru* status. The final diversion takes in Vaux, the village that was the model for the *Clochemerle* books.

Les Pierres Dorées

The 'golden stones' or *pierres dorées* circuit wanders vaguely for some 50 km (30 miles). Here the main attractions are the beautiful scenery, the castles at Jarnioux and Châtillon d'Azergues and a liberal selection of tasting cellars, many attached to co-operative cellars.

Tasting cellars and restaurants

There is no shortage of opportunity to taste the wines of the Beaujolais. Round every corner there seems to be a tasting cellar. There are also many fine restaurants specializing in the simple, but hearty, food of the neighbourhood. Here the motto could be, 'Eat, drink and be merry' with no thought for tomorrow.

Close at hand, too, is the city of Lyon, whose restaurants are renowned throughout the world of fine food. A local saying has it that it is watered by three rivers, the Rhône, the Saône, and the Beaujolais!

The village of Fleurie has a fine reputation for its charcuterie *as well as its wine. Indeed, the co-operative cellar was founded by Monsieur Chabert, who combined the roles of pork butcher and* vigneron.

FOOD IN BURGUNDY

The diversity of the wines of Burgundy is matched by the diversity of its foods, and wine sauces form an essential part of the cookery, be it the white wines, for dishes like *Jambon* (ham) *au Chablis*, or the reds for *Coq au Chambertin* or *Oeufs en Meurette*.

Burgundy is rich in its raw materials. The river Saône and its tributaries provide plenty of coarse fish for such traditional dishes as the *Pochouse*, of Verdun sur le Doubs. From beyond the river come Bresse chickens, with their distinctive yellowish flesh and rich texture, from their diet of maize. There are also the waterfowl of the Dombes.

Charolais beef gives magnificent steaks and the base for that dish that never seems to succeed so well elsewhere, Boeuf Bourguignon. The forests of the Morvan and the Châtillonnais offer venison and wild boar to go with the fullest-bodied wines of the Côte de Nuits.

The snails of Burgundy, too, are without rival, though their collection is now strictly limited.

Finally, Burgundy is proud of its cheeses. From north-west of Dijon comes Epoisses, often aged in the local brandy. The monks of Cîteaux make a tangy cow's-milk cheese. There are goat's-milk cheeses made throughout the region, perhaps the best-known being the Chevreton de Mâcon, but, if you can find it, try the rare Claquebitou of the Hautes-Côtes.

ROMANECHE-THORINS
Les Vins Georges Duboeuf 71570 Romanèche-Thorins. Tel:85 35 51 13. Mon-Fri 080–1230,1330–1730 Sat 0800–1230. TF.WS.E.

ST ETIENNE-DES-OULLIERES
Château des Tours St Etienne la Varenne, 69460 St Etienne-des-Oullières. Tel:47 03 40 86. Mon-Fri 0800–1200,1400–1800. TF.WS.E.

SALLES-ARBUISSONAS
G.A.E.C. René et Christian Miolane Le Cellier, 69460 Salles-Arbuissonas. Tel:47 67 52 67 or 74 67 52 74. Mon-Sat by appointment only. TF (with purchase) WS.E. Audio-visual show, collection of wine implements.

The Rhône

Since before Roman times, the valley of the Rhône has been one of the great highways of the civilized world. As with many highways, most who pass along it are mainly interested in reaching their destination and pay little heed to what is on either side. The wines of the Rhône, however, deserve more attention, for their individuality and quality. The Rhône is one of the greatest wine rivers of the world. Near its source, in Switzerland, are produced the sensational wines of the Valais. After it leaves Lake Geneva and flows westwards, it passes through Savoie where the sparkling wines of Seyssel are made. However it is only after it joins the Saône at Lyons and turns southward that it concerns us in this book.

In the next 230km (143 miles), as far as Avignon, some of the finest wines in the world are made; wines like Côte Rôtie and Hermitage, Tavel and Muscat de Beaumes-de-Venise.

Amongst the finest vineyards producing Côtes-du-Rhône-Villages lies the 12th-century château of Suze-la-Rousse. Here has been established the Université du Vin, which gives courses on the wines of France throughout the year.

There are three main roads down the valley of the Rhône. On the west bank there is the N86, on the east the N7, and then the motorway, the A7.

Of these three roads, it is the first that is the route of the dedicated vineyard visitor, for driving south from Lyon it is on that side of the river that he will find all the well-known vineyards as far as Tournon. It is not, however, a fast road and if your time is limited, it is probably better to use the motorway and take the most convenient exit for the vineyards you want to see: Vienne South for Côte-Rotie and Condrieu; Tournon for Hermitage; and Orange for Châteauneuf-du-Pape.

While the Rhône valley is perhaps best known for its full-bodied red wines, the area does produce a surprising selection and variety. As well as the reds, there are also fine dry white wines (in Victorian times, white Hermitage was considered to be one of the great wines of the world), excellent rosés like Tavel and Lirac, sparkling wine from Saint-Péray and luscious dessert wines, like the Muscats of Beaume-de-Venise.

There is one wine that is produced along almost the full length of the vineyards, and that is simple Côtes du Rhône. For the most part this is red wine, though white and rosé wines are also made. The most common grape variety is the Grenache, but others are used as necessary.

Vienne

The town of Vienne lies some 30km (19 miles) south of Lyon and it is just south of here that the Rhône vineyards begin. Vienne is one of the oldest cities of France, dating back to long before Roman times. There are the remains of a temple dedicated to the Emperor Augustus and his wife Livia and there is a tradition that Hannibal left the Rhône valley here on his trans-Alpine journey. Vienne played an important role in early Christian history and one can still read the Epistle of the Martyrs of Vienne to their colleagues in the eastern Church.

Côte Rôtie

Just south of Vienne, on the other bank of the river, are the vineyards of Côte Rôtie. These are among the steepest in France and the vines are planted in a unique fashion: three separate vines on individual poles which meet together at the top.

The two main slopes are called the Côte Brune and the Côte Blonde, in memory of the two beautiful daughters of a local nobleman. Most Côte Rôtie is a blend from the two sources. At the foot of the vineyards is the town of Ampuis, home to many of the growers and merchants.

To get to the Rhône
Vienne is 490km (306 miles) from Paris and 92km (57 miles) from Mâcon on the A6 and A7 motorways. Orange is 657km (410 miles) from Paris and 259km (162 miles) from Mâcon.

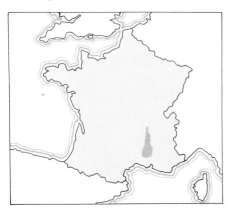

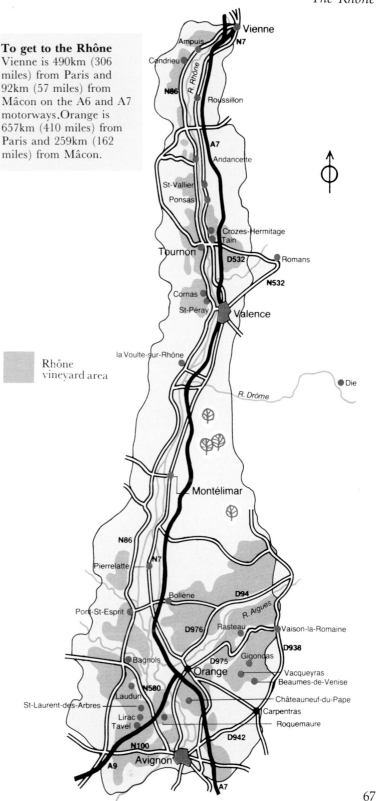

Rhône vineyard area

CHATEAU GRILLET
Neyret-Gachet Château Grillet, 42410 Verin. Tel:74 59 51 56. By appointment only. WS.E.

CONDRIEU
Georges Vernay 1 rte Nationale, 69420 Condrieu. Tel:74 59 52 22. (M. Georges or M. Luc Vernay) Every day 0900–1900. TP. WS.

COTE ROTIE
S.A. J.Vidal-Fleury Route Nationale, 69420 Ampuis. Tel:74 56 10 18. (M. J P Rochias) Mon-Fri 0800–1200, 1400–1800. Closed 3 weeks in Jul. TF (at their discretion).WS.E.

SERRIERES
Cave St Desirat 07340 Serrières. Tel:75 34 22 05. (M. Chaleat). Every day 0900– 1200, 1400–1800. TP.WS.E. Audio-visual presentation, picnic area.

Condrieu
Five km (3 miles) further along the road from Côte Rôtie comes the village of Condrieu. This is renowned for its long-lasting white wine of the same name, made from the rare Viognier grape, found almost nowhere else in the world but this short stretch of the Rhône valley. It reaches its peak in the wines of Château Grillet, a vineyard which has its own microclimate and the smallest production of any single *appellation contrôlée* in France. The rarity of both Condrieu and Château Grillet means that they are not cheap, but their individual, luscious, sunny, fruity, yet dry, flavour should not be missed.

Ardèche
On the western bank of the river come the, almost entirely, red wines of Saint-Joseph, from the Syrah grape. We are now in the Ardèche department and it is here that many experimental plantings have been

made with 'foreign' grapes like the Gamay and the Chardonnay. The famous Burgundy house of Louis Latour, for example, has planted in the region, because of the comparative cheapness of the land and the favourable climate. Because the wines are not made from the traditional grape varieties, they do not have *appellation contrôlée* status, but that of *vin de pays*. Many of these are of excellent quality.

On the other bank of the river is the town of Saint-Vallier, which was once a centre of the silk trade. Just to the south, the village of Ponsas is overlooked by a rocky cliff, called Pilate's Castle, as the legend has it that Pontius Pilate committed suicide by jumping off it.

Hermitage
No one would claim that the twin towns of Tain and Tournon are attractive, but above them rises the stark hillside famous for Hermitage wine. There have been vines planted

The steep hillside vineyard of one of the greatest red wines of France, Côte Rôtie, originally planted in Roman times. One of the major owners is the company of E. Guigal, based in the nearby town of Ampuis.

here for more than two thousand years, despite Celtic claims that they were first planted by St Patrick. The hill gets its name, however, from Gaspard de Stérimberg, who retired to a cell on the summit, having been wounded after fighting the Albigensian heretics in 1224.

There are two distinct types of soil on the hill: granitic for the red grapes, and clayey for the white. The exposure to the sun ensures that exceptionally full-bodied wines are made, which are capable of lasting for decades.

Traditionally, there are a number of differently named sites on the hill, each giving a wine with its individual character. Occasionally, these can be found as individual wines, but more often they are blended together to produce the perfect whole.

Crozes-Hermitage and Cornas

Eleven villages surrounding the hill of Hermitage have the right to call their wine Crozes-Hermitage. While there is a relationship in style with its illustrious neighbour, it is not as close as the growers would have you believe; the reds might age well, but the whites are certainly best drunk young.

Returning to the other side of the river, opposite the important town of Valence, there are two small areas producing fine wines. The first of these is Cornas. Again, the vineyards are on steep slopes and the combination of soil and microclimate

Whilst the Rhône Valley is particularly known for its red wines, it also produces some excellent white wines. Of these, the rarest and most expensive is Château Grillet, made from the Viognier grape.

Nougat being prepared in copper vessels at the Fabrique de Suprême Nougat, Montélimar (which will admit visitors bringing a copy of this book).

BEAUMES-DE-VENISE
Caves des Vignerons de Beaumes-de-Venise 84190 Beaumes-de-Venise. Tel:90 62 94 45. (M. Goria) Mon-Fri 0900–1200, 1400–1800. TF.WS.E.

GIGONDAS
G.A.E.C. du Domaine St Gayan Gayan, 84190 Gigondas. Tel:90 65 86 33. (M. or Mme Meffre) Every day 0900–1145, 1400–1900. TF.WS.

ORANGE
Chambovet Père et Fils S.A. rue St Jean Prolongée, 84100 Orange. Tel:90 34 21 80. (Mme Claudine Chambovet-Duval) Mon-Fri 0800–1200, 1300–1730. TF.WS.E. Three estates in Côtes du Rhône.

gives perhaps the biggest wine of the Rhône. As one English writer has said, 'A good Cornas one or two years old is a savage, dark wine that leaves the eye impressed and the palate coloured.'

Two sparkling wines
The reputation of the wines of Saint-Péray goes back to classical times. Traditionally still and white, four-fifths are now sparkling, made in the same way as Champagne. Murray's *Handbook for France*, dated 1884, suggests that the visitor to Valence

PRODUIT DE FRANCE

CONDRIEU

APPELLATION CONDRIEU CONTROLÉE

Mis en bouteille à la Propriété   750 ml

Georges VERNAY, VITICULTEUR A CONDRIEU (Rhône)

should 'Try here the sparkling wine of St Péray, an excellent wine, not inferior to Champagne, 3 or 4fr the bottle.' The price may have changed, but not the quality.

The other sparkling wine of the region, Clairette de Die, comes from some 65km (40 miles) away on the other side of the Rhône, on one of its tributaries, the Drôme. Here two styles of wine are made: a *brut*, by the traditional champagne method, and the sweeter variety where the sparkle in the bottle comes from a naturally delayed first fermentation.

Coteaux de Tricastin
After Valence, there is a coda in the vineyards of the Rhône lasting some 70km (43 miles). It is not until after Montélimar, renowned for its nougat, that, on the left bank of the Rhône, begin the vineyards of the Coteaux de Tricastin. Here the land is stony and poor, continually scoured by the Mistral, and it is only in the last 30 years that vines have been replanted since they were destroyed by phylloxera. Much of the planting has been carried out by *pieds noirs* (ex-colonials from Algeria). The wines, mainly red, are very similar to Côtes du Rhône.

Orange
Beyond the riverside nuclear power-station at Pierrelatte, the vineyards producing Côtes du Rhône begin again and it is from the three *départements* of Drôme, Vaucluse and Gard that the bulk of it comes. At the centre of the region is the town of Orange, the scene of an annual wine fair, held in the Roman amphitheatre.

For many years, Orange was the capital of a small independent principality, which was not integrated into France until the Treaty of Utrecht in 1713. It also gave its name to William of Orange. Remains include a Roman triumphal arch on the northern side of the town and traces of a Roman circus.

To the north-east lie a number of villages that have traditionally sold their wine as simple Côtes du Rhône, or the superior Côtes du Rhône Villages. Some of these have progressed above this status. Gigondas, where there are the remains of a castle belonging to the Princes of Orange, had the good fortune to be the home of two wine merchants intent on promoting the local wines and in 1971 was rewarded with full *appellation contrôlée* status for its red wines. Vacqueyras, its neighbour, has since followed in its footsteps.

Rasteau, on the other hand, has built its reputation on a fortified wine made in the same way as port, but from the Grenache grape.

Beaumes-de-Venise

Better known is the Muscat de Beaumes-de-Venise. Beaumes-de-Venise was a spa in Roman times and has had a reputation for its wines for many centuries.

No one knows when the Muscat was first planted. (This is almost the

VACQUEYRAS
Caves des Vignerons de Vacqueyras 84190 Vacqueyras. Every day 0900–1200, 1400–1700. TF.WS.
Domaine de Fourmone rte de Bollène, 84190 Vacqueyras. Tel:90 65 86 05. Every day 0900–1200, 1400–1900. TF.WS.

One of the delights of the vineyards of the Rhône are the dessert wines made from the Muscat grape, particularly round Beaumes-de-Venise. Here the super-ripe grapes are being picked.

only place where it can be found in the Rhône valley.) Certainly its rich fruitiness seems to have a wider appeal than most other wines of its type made in France.

Overlooking the vineyards of Gigondas and Vacqueyras is Mont Ventoux. Along its southern slopes run the vineyards of Côtes du Ventoux. A little white wine is made, but most of the production is of a soft, easy drinking red wine.

Châteauneuf-du-Pape

Orange is one of the five communes which together produce perhaps the best-known wine of the Rhône valley, Châteauneuf-du-Pape. There is no doubt that much of the historic reputation of this wine is due to the fact that when the Popes left Rome and established themselves in nearby Avignon during the 14th century they did much to promote the local wines. It was at

Châteauneuf that they built their summer palace and there are still some remains of this.

The complexity of the wine of Châteauneuf is due largely to the fact that up to 13 different grape varieties may be used in its production, each adding a touch of colour to the final picture. The soil is closely covered with large rounded stones and the closely pruned vines benefit from an inverted form of night storage heating: the stones retain through the night much of the heat that they have picked up during the day, and pass it on to the vines.

The local growers have been in the forefront of supporting legislation to protect the quality of their wines. Many of them, in a form of regional pride, have adopted a special bottle, bearing the papal coat of arms on its shoulder. ·

Châteauneuf is best known for its red wines, which are full-bodied and capable of long ageing, but it also produces small quantities of an excellent white wine.

CHATEAUNEUF-DU-PAPE
Caves St Pierre rte d'Avignon, 84320 Châteauneuf-du-Pape. Tel:90 83 72 14. Mon-Fri 0930–1130, 1400–1700. Closed Aug. TF.WS.E.
Château Mont-Redon rte D68, 84230 Châteauneuf-du-Pape. Tel:90 83 72 75. 0800–1200, 1400–1800. TF (at their discretion) WS.
Domaine de la Rocquette 2 ave Louis Pasteur, 84320 Châteauneuf du Pape. Jun-Sep every day 0900–1200,1400–1800. TF.WS.E.
Paul Avril Clos des Papes, 84320 Châteauneuf-du-Pape. Tel:90 83 70 13. (Mme Nicolai) Mon-Fri 0900–1130, 1400–1700. TF.WS.E.

Wherever fruit, including grapes, is grown in France, spirits are distilled, often by a mobile still which moves from village to village. Here is a retired example, from Châteauneuf-du-Pape, almost 70 years old.

Avignon

The history of Avignon is closely linked to the period during which seven Popes, and three anti-Popes, lived there. The church purchased the city by some rather sharp practice. Joanna of Naples, who was still a minor, was persuaded to sell it for the sum of 80,000 gold crowns. Rather sadly, she never received the money, though the Popes had already taken possession of the city. When the Popes returned to Rome, it remained part of their possessions, being governed by a Papal Legate. Indeed, it did not finally become part of France until after the French Revolution.

Having had as many as 80,000 inhabitants during the 17th century, the population was less than half that a hundred years ago. It is only quite recently that it has returned to its previous glory.

There is much to see in the town. It is still surrounded by 14th-century battlements with 39 watch towers. The former Palace of the Popes has been at various times a military barracks and even a prison. This must have been a great come-down from the days of luxurious extravagance and debauchery that marked the times of the Papal court.

Sur le pont...

Dancing on the bridge at Avignon, or at least on the 800 year-old Pont Saint Bénézet, is now strictly limited, as only four out of the original 19 arches remain. On it, there is the small chapel of St Nicholas, which holds the remains of the saint who gave the bridge his name.

Behind the church of St Didier, the narrow rue du Roi René has a number of beautiful old buildings.

The typical Rhône vineyard village of Gigondas, with its flattened red-tiled roofs. Here are produced full-bodied, warming red wines.

To the north-west of Avignon are the Côtes du Rhône vineyards of the Gard *département*. These are particularly known for their rosé wines. The west bank of the Rhône, here, presents a totally different outlook to the east. Instead of a picture of rich greens, there is the drab grey aridity of the *garrigues* (areas of rough, stony countryside)

AIGUES-MORTES
Listel Domaine de Jarras, 30220 Aigues-Mortes. Tel:66 53 63 65. Easter-30 Jun every day 1000–1830 1 Jul-30 Sep every day 1000–1900 1 Oct-Easter Mon-Fri 0900–1130, 1400–1730 Sat 0900–1130. TF.WS.E. Historic cellars, video, picnic area.

CHUSCLAN
Caves des Vignerons de Chusclan 30200 Chusclan. Tel:66 90 11 03. (M. Grandjean) Mon-Sat 0830–1200, 1400–1830. TF.WS.E. Collection of wine implements, picnic area.

LIRAC
Comte de Régis Château de Segriès, 30126 Lirac. Tel:66 21 85 35. (M. de Régis) TF. Wine on sale at Caveau de la Fontaine in Lirac.

On the west bank of the Rhône, the historic port of Roquemaure lies in the centre of the appellation of Lirac.

baked by the sun and tormented by the wind. The soil is basically chalky, but is covered by layers of flat, flaking stones, which, as in Châteauneuf, reflect the heat.

Two of the villages, Chusclan and Laudun, have the appellation Côtes du Rhône Villages, but two others, Tavel and Lirac, have their own individual appellations.

Tavel has long had the reputation of producing the finest rosé wine in France. In Britain and the United States, where the consumption of rosé wine represents only a small fraction of the total, this may not appear a very important title, but in France, where a lot is drunk, Tavel is held in high esteem.

Much of the vineyard area was allowed to return to scrubland after the phylloxera plague, and it is only during the last thirty years or so that the vineyards of Tavel have taken on a new lease of life with extensive replanting. Much of the initiative for this has come from the local co-operative, which has the reputation of being one of the most dynamic and conscientious in France.

Wine from Lirac
Four villages have the right to make Lirac wine. Of these, Saint-Laurent-des-Arbres is perhaps the most attractive, with an early fortified church. Roquemaure, too, has a long history, claiming a supporting role in the Hannibal story.

Castles in the air
Whilst Lirac was best known for its rosé wines, an ever-increasing quantity of red wine is now being made. Regular attenders at French wine fairs, the Pons-Mure family came to the region after Algerian independence. Not having a château to put on their labels, they decided to call their wine Castel Oualou, which, I gather, is Arabic for the castle that does not exist or, perhaps, castle in the air. To complete the image, they added some turrets straight out of Walt Disney. This did not appeal to the sense of humour of the local authorities and they asked for them to be removed. Instead, the family put a broad cross across the fairytale castle – and that is how the labels look to this day!

Pont du Gard
It is about here that the vineyards of the Côte du Rhône finish, but one short excursion that is well worth making from Avignon is to the Pont du Gard. This is some 22km (14 miles) west of the town, beyond

FOOD IN THE RHONE

It is difficult to write about the food specialities of the Rhône, for gastronomically it is not one area. Indeed, whilst driving down it, you cross the great boundary in French gastronomy; on one side the cooking is done with butter and on the other with olive oil.

In the north, Lyon is one of the gastronomic centres of France, known for its sausages, like *rosétte* and *judas*, its tripe and dishes like *la poularde demi-deuil*, chicken in cream with truffles.

Down the valley of the Rhône, there are a number of seasonal fruit markets for apricots, nectarines and, near Carpentras, melons. The Ardèche is known for its chestnuts and the Drôme for its herbs, honey and thrush patés. For a sticky finale, the best nougat in the world comes from Montélimar.

Remoulins on the N100. The Pont is a magnificent Roman aqueduct, in three tiers, 48 metres (160 feet) above the valley of the river Gardon. The channel to carry the water is more than 2 metres (7 feet) deep and over a metre (4 feet) wide. Just 20km (12½ miles) further on is the magnificent city of Nîmes.

While we have come to the end of the vineyards of the Côtes du Rhône, there are still what might be called some 'Rhône' vineyards in the region of the Costières du Gard, on the western fringes of the Rhône delta. Here most of the wine that is made is red, though there is also some rosé and a little white.

More special is the white Clairette de Bellegarde, from south-east of Nîmes, which has its own *appellation contrôlée*. The production is very small; the wine is dry, with a flowery flavour and little acidity.

More common, perhaps because the village that gives it its name straddles the main N113 road, is Muscat de Lunel. This, as it suggests, is a sweet fortified wine made from the muscat grape. It lacks, for the most part, the finesse of flavour that one finds in the similar wines from Beaumes-de-Venise.

Where the river Rhône reaches the Mediterranean, the deposit that it has carried down has created a vast sandy delta, the Camargue, noted for its bulls, horses and flamingoes. This seems the most unlikely place for vineyards to be planted, but it is here that one finds one of the biggest vineyard companies in France, Les Salins du Midi.

As its name suggests, this company has traditionally made its money from salt; indeed, it still does so. In a bid to diversify and to use land that otherwise would have no commercial application, it has planted along the coast from Sète eastwards, almost to the mouth of the Rhône more than 1,600 hectares (almost 4,000 acres) of vines. Here a broad range of wines is made with the appellation of Vin de Pays des Sables du Golfe du Lion. The largest of these properties, the Domaine de Jarras, lies on the main D979 road from Aigues-Mortes to le Grau-du-Roi.

It seems fitting that our journey through the vineyards of the Rhône Valley should finish here in the mediaeval walled town of Aigues-Mortes, for it was from here that St Louis set out on his own pilgrimage, crusades to the Holy Land.

TAVEL
G.A.E.C. Domaine Maby
30126 Tavel. Tel:66 50 03 40. Mon-Fri 0800–1200, 1330–1800. Closed 1st fortnight in Aug. TF.WS.E.
Les Vignerons de Tavel
30126 Tavel. Tel:66 50 03 57. Every day 0800–1200, 1400–1900. TF.WS.E.

FOR FURTHER INFORMATION
C.I.C.D.R. Maison du Tourisme et du Vin, 41, Cours Jean-Jaurès, 84000 Avignon. Tel:90 86 47 09.

Wine festivals
Côte Rôtie wine fair, Ampuis, 3rd Sun June.
Orange wine fair mid June.
Festival of St Marc, about 25 Apr, Châteauneuf-du-Pape.
Côte du Rhône Villages fair, end May, Vacqueyras.
Lirac wine fair, end May, Roquemaure.
Cornas wine fair, about 7 Dec.

The Loire Valley

The Loire is the longest river in France, with its source lying no more than 40 km (25 miles) from the valley of the river Rhône, south of Valence. Along its path are created many of the finest white wines in the world – and many of the lesser, but no less enjoyable reds.

It is a gentle river; it does not have the commercial importance of such other wine-rivers as the Rhine and the Rhône. It is a beautiful river, with its many châteaux and historic towns. Indeed, there is almost too much of it to absorb at one time and the wine-lover always runs the risk of being diverted. For this reason alone, there is much to be said for trying to digest it one piece at a time, first perhaps the Muscadet, then Anjou, then Touraine. . . .

Although the main vineyard areas of the Loire valley are concentrated in three regions – Touraine, Anjou and the Muscadet – wine is made almost all along its length and that of its tributaries. The intrepid tourist will nearly always be able to find a local wine to drink. Not far from Lyon are the red wines of the Côte Roannaise and the Côtes du Forez made from the Gamay grape. For those taking the cure at Vichy, there is some relief to be had in the wines of Saint-Pourçain-sur-Sioule.

For the convenience of the motorist, we have already attached the great wines of Pouilly-sur-Loire and Sancerre to the vineyards of Burgundy. To their west are three small vineyard regions, all making dry white wines from the Sauvignon grape: Menetou-Salon, Reuilly and

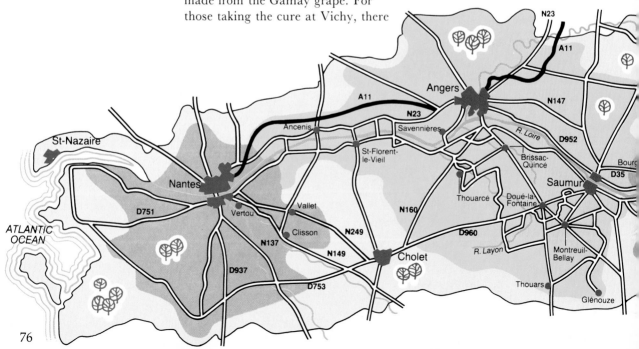

Quincy. The wine from the last can have a pronounced farmyard flavour. The other two also make some rosé wine from the Pinot Noir.

Again to the west, to the south of the river Cher, Valençay produces a range of light wines, for local drinking. Downstream from Sancerre are made Coteaux du Giennois and Vin de l'Orléannais.

Vin de Pays du Jardin de la France

This wine is produced throughout the Loire Valley as red, white and rosé. Often it is made from experimental plantings of grapes that are not traditional to the area. Unless there is an informative label, you may not know what to expect, for this is a catch-all appellation. Nevertheless, it is generally a good buy.

Muscadet

Anjou

Chinon and Bourgeuil

Touraine

Quincy and Reuilly

Sancerre and Pouilly-sur-Loire

Giennois

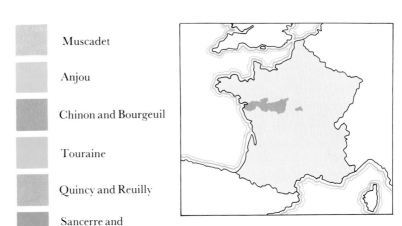

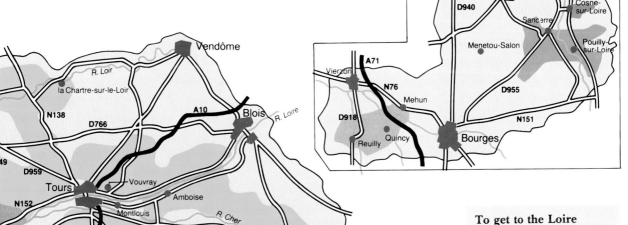

To get to the Loire
From Paris, Tours is 234km (146 miles) by the A10 motorway and Nantes, 380km (237 miles) by the A11, N23 and A11 again. From the Channel ports, Tours is 234km (146 miles) from Caen by the D514, N158 and N138 and Nantes is 155km (97 miles) from Saint-Malo by the N137.

Touraine

The city of Tours has much to offer visitors. It is an easy drive from Paris, it has many good hotels and restaurants and it has vineyards and châteaux on its doorstep.

In wine history, the town is important because of the Abbey of St Martin of Tours, which for many years effectively ran the town. It had a number of dependent monasteries throughout France and the order was responsible for the establishment of many mediaeval wine domains.

St Martin

The connection of St Martin with the noble science of drinking is close, for drunkenness is still described as 'the illness of St Martin', and a bacchic celebration is held in his name each year in late January. He is also credited with having planted the first vineyard in Vouvray. Given the number of vinous miracles in his name, it seems impossible that the local wines could have existed

The village of Chambord boasts one of the most imposing, if not the most beautiful, châteaux of the Loire.

On the River Cher, in the heart of the vineyards of Touraine, lies the village of Pouillé. Here red wines are made from the Cabernet Franc and the Gamay, and whites from the Chenin and Sauvignon.

without him. Little remains of the Abbey apart from the Tour du Trésor and part of the cloister.

The church of St Julien dates from the beginning of the 13th century. For some time, until the middle of the last century it was used as a coach-house. Now it has been fully restored and honour is given where due: in the cloister is an old wine-press. It is also worth visiting the Cathedral of St Gatien.

Châteaux of the Loire

Visits to some of the beautiful châteaux of the region can be combined with those to cellars, but it may be wise to mention them separately. It is difficult to know which to choose, but three that are within easy driving of Tours, and which could be visited in the same day, are Chambord, Amboise and Chenonceaux.

Chambord is the furthest away, being 16 kms (10 miles) east of Blois, on the southern side of the Loire. Built by François I, it is an impressive building, with 444 rooms. Amboise is by far the oldest of the three châteaux, being built on a rock

The cellars of well-known merchants, Marc Brédif, at Rochecorbon. Here, historic vintages of Vouvray are kept in this cellar cut into the tufa cliffs, alongside the River Loire.

VOUVRAY

Ets. Marc Brédif 87 Quai de la Loire, Rochecorbon, 37210 Vouvray. Tel:47 52 50 07. (M. Marchalot) Visits Mon-Fri 1030 and 1600. TP.WS.E. Rock cellars.

Prince Philippe Pontiatowski le Clos Boudouin, Vallée de Nouy, 37210 Vouvray. Tel:47 52 71 02. (M. or Mme Penilleau) Mon-Fri 0800–1200, 1400–1800. 15 Aug-10 Sep. TF.WS.E (if the Prince is there).

FOR FURTHER INFORMATION
C.I.V.T. 19 Square Prosper Merimée, 37000 Tours. Tel:47 05 40 01.

Wine festivals
Vouvray wine festival, last Sat Jan.
Montlouis wine fair, last Sat Feb.
Amboise wine fair, Easter.
Vouvray wine fair, and Amboise wine fair, mid Aug.

overlooking the town and having for long been the residence of the Kings of France. Stories attached to it are numerous, but amongst the less agreeable is that of the year 1560, when the Duc de Guise had almost twelve hundred Protestants executed for plotting against him. The bodies were then hung from the castle walls and the streets of the town were said to be streaming with blood. The executioner resigned because of overwork and the royal court fled the town because of the smell.

Chenonceaux is rather happier; being the scene of the extravagant love-affair between Henri II and Diane de Poitiers. It escaped destruction at the time of the Revolution, because of the respect accorded to the then owner, the literary widow, Mme Dupin, who had counted Bolingbroke, Rousseau and Voltaire among her friends.

To the east of Tours, there are two vineyard areas of note, Vouvray and Montlouis.

Vouvray

The vineyards of Vouvray begin, just 6km (4 miles) from the centre of the town, on the north bank of the Loire. Here there are low chalk cliffs standing back from the river into which have been dug extensive wine cellars and, occasionally, houses.

The wines of Vouvray are all white and are all made from the Chenin Blanc grape. Nevertheless, there is a remarkably broad range of styles, ranging from wines that are bone-dry to, in the best years, wines that are sweet, with a honey-like opulence. In addition, classic sparkling wines are made by the Champagne method.

On the south bank of the river, almost opposite, lie the vineyards of Montlouis, a self-styled *Capitale du Vin*. The wines were for long sold as Vouvray and are similar but lighter.

While the two areas lie on opposite banks of the Loire, be warned, there is no road bridge between them and the motorist must either return to Tours or go on to Amboise to cross.

Chinon and Bourgeuil

BOURGEUIL
Maison Audebert et Fils
ave Jean Causeret, 37140
Bourgeuil. Tel:47 97 70 06.
(M. Jean-Claude
Audebert) Mon-Fri
0900–1200,1330–1830.
Closed Sat-Sun (except by
prior appointment)
TF.WS.E. Historic cellars,
collection of wine
implements.
Régis Mureau La
Gaucherie, Ingrandes de
Touraine, 37140 Bourgeuil.
Every day Closed 2nd half
of Jul. TF.WS.

CHINON
Couly Dutheil 12 rue
Diderot, 37500 Chinon.
Tel:47 93 05 82. Tue-Fri
0900–1200,1400–1700.
TF.WS.E. Rock cellars.
Maison Plouzeau et Fils
94 rue Haute St Maurice,
37500 Chinon. Tel:47 93 16
34. (M. Pierre Plouzeau)
Apr-Oct Mon-Sat
0900–1200,1400–1800.
TP.WS. Rock cellars-under
the Château de Chinon.
S.C.E.A. Charles Joguet
Sazilly, 37220 l'Ile
Bouchard. Tel:47 58 55 53.
(Charles Joguet or Alain
Delaunay) Mon 1400–1800
Tue-Fri 0800–1200,1400–
1800. TF.WS.

Wine festivals
Wine fair in Bourgueil and
St Nicolas de Bourgueil, 1st
weekend Feb.
Azay-le-Rideau wine fair,
last Sat in Feb.
Wine fair in Bourgueil and
St Nicolas de Bourgueil,
Easter.

The Loire is a river of white wines, but there are red wines made, and good red wines, too. Those with the highest reputation come from three towns to the west of Tours, Chinon, Bourgueil and Saint-Nicolas-de Bourgueil.

Chinon
To get to Chinon, the best way is to take the D751, south-west from Tours. After 23km (15 miles), you come to Azay-le-Rideau, which has the right to add its name to that of Touraine for its wines. The majority of these are dry and semi-sweet white wines made from the Chenin Blanc, though there is also a little light rosé made.

The village is, however, much better known for its château, which like so many others in the area, was built during the reign of François I. From there the road passes through a large forest before arriving at Chinon, a town steeped in history.

Most of the town is squeezed between the river Vienne and a steep hill on which there are the remains of a substantial castle. It was here that Joan of Arc came to offer her aid to the Dauphin and where she was given her suit of armour by the King of France.

On the other side of the river are the village of Seuilly, where Rabelais was born, and Fontevraud, where Richard the Lionheart died.

There is a minute quantity of white Chinon made, but it is the red wines that are of interest. These are made from the Cabernet Franc grape, a lesser relative of the famous Cabernet Sauvignon. Local legend has it that the grape was brought from Bordeaux by Cardinal Richelieu. It gives a light, rather grassy wine,

which generally can be drunk young and is often more agreeable served lightly chilled.

In Chinon, two styles of wine are made. From the hillsides, where there is a subsoil of porous tufa, a firmer, full-bodied wine is made. This can benefit from ageing for three or four years. From the vineyards on the plain, where the soil is a mixture of sand and gravel, lighter, fresher wines are made, which can be drunk young. The wines of Chinon all have a certain crisp acidity and fresh raspberry flavour.

Bourgeuil
On the north side of the Loire, 17km (10 miles) from Chinon is Bourgueil, a rather drab, grey village. It has a Benedictine monastery, and, not to be outdone by their neighbours and rivals at Chinon, the growers of Bourgueil claim that the Cabernet Franc was first planted in the region by one of the abbots, five and a half centuries before Richelieu arrived on the scene.

The vineyards are protected on the north by a high wooded plateau, the Landes Saint-Martin, and because of this have a particularly mild climate with low rainfall.

This rather special situation has meant that wine is not the sole source of income of most of the local growers, many of whom also plant soft fruits and vegetables for the local markets of Tours and Angers. Nevertheless, it is an area which shows few outward signs of wealth though no shortage of hospitality. The vines are on three different types of soil, the sandy valley bottom, a gravelly broad flat strip called the *terrasse*, from where most of the wine comes, and the south-facing slopes.

It is from here that the finest wines come, though the grower will usually blend the wines from vineyards on the differing soils.

While it is hard to generalize, the wines of Bourgueil tend to lack the immediate charm of those of Chinon. They are rather more dour and austere, especially when they are very young. They are, however, fuller-bodied and will age better.

Saint-Nicolas-de-Bourgeuil

The last of this trio of red wines, Saint-Nicolas-de-Bourgeuil, has gained its independence from its neighbour for reasons that no one seems prepared to explain. It is true that the soil tends to be rather poorer, which is not a bad thing for the making of wine, and that the permitted yield is rather lower, but otherwise there is little to differentiate it.

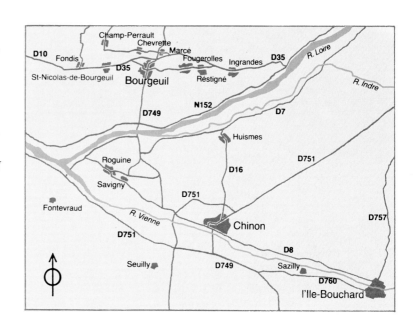

The 16th-century Château of Azay-le-Rideau is one of the most beautiful along the length of the Loire. In the neighbourhood are made crisp white and rosé wines, whose success is restricted by the very limited quantities that are made.

Anjou

If there were to be a celestial Wine Olympics and each wine region was allocated only three entries, there is little doubt that all the three chosen to represent the Loire would come from Anjou. This is the heartland of Loire viticulture and it is here that the Chenin Blanc, called locally Pineau de la Loire, produces its finest wines.

It seems sad that many drinkers' total knowledge of the local wines has been the ubiquitous rosé d'Anjou or its slightly upmarket brother Cabernet d'Anjou. Both slightly sweet, they are in no way typical of what the area can produce. Indeed, demand for both has fallen to such an extent that the growers are now using the grapes for making fresh, red wines. The consumption of dry Anjou blanc is also on the increase.

Angers

These are the wines that are produced widely throughout the area, but there are a number of individual vineyard areas that should be visited, and the attractive town of Angers makes a useful base for this. The dominant feature here is the Château, which has been described as the 'finest feudal castle in France'. Built overlooking the River Maine by Philippe-Auguste and completed by St Louis, it has served as a prison for a broad variety of people.

The other building that stands out over the town is the Cathedral of St Maurice. Much of it dates from the 12th century. From the 14th century come the remarkable series of tapestries picturing the Apocalypse in realistic detail.

What is now the *préfecture* used to be the convent of St Aubin. This has a remarkable late Roman arcade.

Each of the arches is decorated with elaborately carved faces in human and animal forms.

Saumur

The second town of Anjou, 44km (27 miles) upstream on the south bank of the Loire, is Saumur. Here, too, history has had an important part to play. For many years it was one of the strongest Protestant towns in France, though for some strange reason it was granted a monopoly of making rosaries. As a result of the revocation of the Edict of Nantes, however, three-quarters of the inhabitants had to emigrate and the town fell on hard times.

In 1793, during the Vendéan revolt, the castle overlooking the town was captured by a small force of only sixty men, led by Henri de Laroche-Jacquelin. He threw his hat into the midst of the enemy, shouted 'Who's going to find it for me?' and leapt in after it. They subsequently captured, one must imagine with some additional help, 60 cannon, 10,000

SAUMUR
Bouvet Ladubay rue de l'Abbaye, St Hilaire St Florent, 49400 Saumur. Tel:41 50 11 12. (Mlle Hériteau) Every day 1000–1200,1430–1800. TF.WS.E. Sparkling wines, audio-visual presentation, rock cellars.

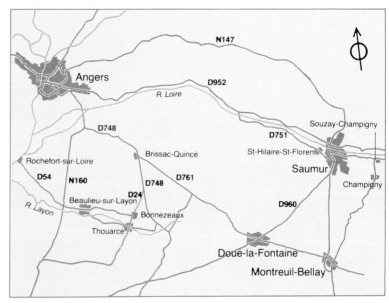

muskets and 11,000 prisoners. The last they released after they had shaved one side of their heads and made them promise not to fight against the Royalists again. With a success like that, one wonders how they ultimately lost!

Saumur now houses the French military cavalry school and there is a museum of equitation in the town.

Just beyond the cavalry school is the suburb of Saint-Hilaire-Saint-Florent, where there are a number of producers of sparkling Saumur. The cellars that they have dug into the hillside are ideal for the ageing of the wine. Indeed, a number of the major Champagne companies have invested heavily in the making of the local 'Champagne method' wines.

On the other side of the town are the vineyards of Saumur-Champigny, which produce a most agreeable fruity red wine from the Cabernet Franc grape. While they have a good reputation and, perhaps, a little more appeal than the wines of Chinon and Bourgueil, I find it difficult to understand the cult status that they appear to have in France at the moment.

The local dry white wines are sold as Saumur and are similar in style to the wines of Vouvray. If they are sweeter, they generally appear under the Coteaux de Saumur label.

The capital of Anjou is the city of Angers, known not just for its wines, but also for Cointreau liqueur. Dominating the town is the magnificent mediaeval castle.

83

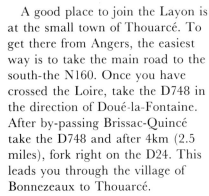

The red wines of Saumur-Champigny, made from the Cabernet Franc grape, are now amongst the most fashionable in France, largely due to their refreshing fruitiness. Here is a typical tasting cellar.

The finest wines of Anjou, and the Loire, come from vineyards south and west of Angers: the sweet wines from the valley of the River Layon, and the dry wines from the vineyards of Savennières on the north bank of the Loire, down country lanes some 16km (10 miles) west of Angers. No one would think in either case that this was a fine wine region, for the best vineyards are not easy to find.

The Layon Valley

The River Layon is remarkable in that it is slow-flowing yet is in quite a deep, winding valley. During its meanderings, the slopes on either side vary considerably in their steepness. As a result of all this, there is a variety of wines made according to the suitability of the individual slope. Where it is steep and faces for the most part towards the south, the sweet Coteaux du Layon is produced; where the slope is less than ideal, Anjou blanc or rosé is made. In two exceptional cases, Bonnezeaux and Quarts de Chaume, something equivalent to *grand cru* status has been awarded.

A good place to join the Layon is at the small town of Thouarcé. To get there from Angers, the easiest way is to take the main road to the south-the N160. Once you have crossed the Loire, take the D748 in the direction of Doué-la-Fontaine. After by-passing Brissac-Quincé take the D748 and after 4km (2.5 miles), fork right on the D24. This leads you through the village of Bonnezeaux to Thouarcé.

Bonnezeaux

The vineyards producing Bonnezeaux are spread along the right bank of the Layon for 2.8km (1.75 miles) in a narrow band. There are three distinct steep slopes: la Montagne, Beauregard and Fesles, separated by narrow valleys. These give a soft, fruity wine with a delicious sweetness, which in the best years will keep, and improve, for many years.

As opposed to the other great wines of the region, Bonnezeaux is not a patrician wine, for it is almost totally produced by a number of small growers in the local villages. As a result, therefore, it represents good value for money for anyone looking for an exceptional sweet wine.

From Thouarcé, you drive through Rablay-sur-Layon and Beaulieu-sur-Layon. When you have crossed the N160 and passed the hamlet of Le Breuil, the other great vineyard of the valley, the Quarts de Chaume, appears on the left.

Here there are just four owners and, as in Sauternes, the picking does not begin until late October, when the noble rot has begun to affect the bunches of grapes.

The pickers will pass through the vines a number of times to pick just

those grapes that have the richest juice.

The vineyard is formed by a series of horseshoes going down to the river. As a result the vines are protected from the wind and there is an ideal micro-climate for the production of such a majestically rich and honeyed wine.

If you continue along the same road and cross the Loire at Rochefort, you immediately arrive at the village of Savennières. Here, the vineyards slope down steeply to the river and the same Chenin Blanc grape gives not sweet wines, but truly great wines that are, for the most part, dry. They have a richness of flavour and complexity of bouquet found in the finest white Burgundies.

Here there are several impressive working châteaux, including those of

The leaves change colour in the Coulée du Serrant vineyard of Savennières. Here are made the greatest dry white wines of the Loire vineyards.

Bizolière, Chamboureau and Epiré. The last makes use of a de-consecrated chapel on the estate as a press-house and wine-cellar.

The two finest vineyards of Savennières are the Coulée du Serrant and La Roche aux Moines. The former is a single walled vineyard, of just under 4 hectares (10 acres) belonging to the dynamic Mme Joly.

The Roche aux Moines is much larger in size, with the vineyards belonging to ten or so different owners. At their best, its wines are capable of rivalling a fine Sauternes, although their style is rather different. These wines are worth seeking out.

BONNEZEAUX
Domaine de Terrebrune
place du Champ de Foire, 49380 Thouarcé. Tel:41 54 01 99. Mon-Sat 0900–1200,1400–1700. TF.WS.E.(with prior notice).

FOR FURTHER INFORMATION
C.I.V.A.S. Hôtel Godeline, 73 rue Plantagenet, 49000 Angers.

Wine festival
Angers wine fair, 1st weekend Jan. Saumur wine fair, 2nd weekend Feb.

Muscadet

ANCENIS
Les Vignerons de Noelle
44150 Ancenis.
Tel:40 98 92 72. Mon-Fri
0800–1215,1315–1800 Sat
0830–1230. TF.WS.E.
Wines from Anjou,
Ancenis and Muscadet.

BASSE-GOULAINE
Marquis de Goulaine
Château de Goulaine,
Haute Goulaine, 44115
Basse-Goulaine. Tel:40 54
91 42. Easter-1 Nov, Sat,
Sun, holidays. 15 Jun-15
Sep 1400–1830. Every day
except Tue. TP.WS.E.
Historic château, butterfly
house.

Strange as it may seem, the
Muscadet vineyards are the nearest
to a Channel port, for if you sail to
Saint-Malo you are only two hours
drive from Nantes.

Nantes

The city of Nantes is built on the
north bank of the Loire. From the
outside, the Cathedral of St Peter is
not very attractive, but among the
works of art inside is a monument to
Francis II, last Duke of Brittany. At
each corner there is a supporter; one
is Temperance with a lantern in one
hand and a horse's bit in the other!

The other major building of the
city is the 14th-century château.

Muscadet – the wine

Within Muscadet there is a
geographical hierarchy. From the
south-east of Nantes comes the
Muscadet de Sèvre et Maine, the
finest wine, which accounts for 85 per
cent of the total. North-east of
Nantes, from around the town of
Ancenis, comes Muscadet des
Coteaux de la Loire, with 5 per cent
of the total. The balance, produced
in peripheral regions, is plain
Muscadet.

Muscadet – the grape

The grape used for all these wines is
also called the Muscadet. It came
from Burgundy, where it is known as
the Melon de Bourgogne, during the
18th century. There is some dispute
as to where it was first planted,
either at the Château de la
Cassemichère at La Chapelle-Heulin,
or at the Clos des Bourguignons at
Clisson.

*Originally from Burgundy, the Melon grape has
now taken the name of the wine it produces, the
Muscadet. Here in the late spring, the vineyards
turn into seas of green.*

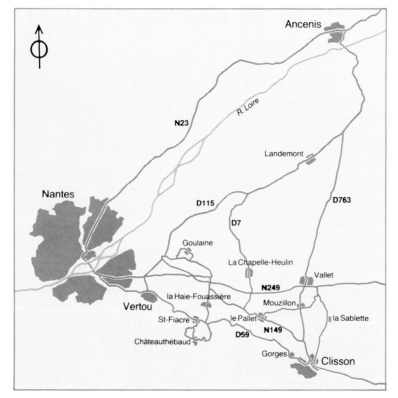

LA CHAPELLE-HEULIN
Donatien-Bahuaud 44330
La Chapelle-Heulin.
Tel:40 06 70 05. (Marie-France Cormerais) Mon-Fri 0900–1200,1400–1700.
TF.WS.E.

ST FIACRE SUR MAINE
Château de Chasseloir
44690 St Fiacre sur Maine.
Tel:40 45 81 15. (M. Pichon) Every day 0800–1800. TF.WS.15th-century tower, historic cellars.
Louis Metaireau La Vevrie, près St Fiacre, 44690 Maison-sur-Sèvre.
Tel:40 54 81 92. (Mlle Marie-Luce Métaireau)
Mon-Fri 0800–1230, 1400–1800 and by appointment.
TP.WS.E.

VALLET
Château des Rois 14 rue des Rois, 44330 Vallet.
Tel:40 33 99 94. (Thérèse Capelle or Nadine Durand) Mon-Fri 0900–1200, 1400–1700.
Sauvion et Fils Château de Cléray, 44330 Vallet.
Tel:40 36 22 55. (Micheline Gerles) Easter-end Sep Mon-Fri 0900–1200, 1400–1700, otherwise by appointment.

Wine museum
Musée Perre Abélard, Chapelle St Michel, Le Pallet, 44330 Vallet. Tel:40 26 40 24. Sat, Sun and holidays 1400–1800 or by appointment with town hall.

FOR FURTHER INFORMATION
C.I.V.O.P.N. Maison des Vins, Bellevue, 44690 la Haye–Fouassière. Tel:40 36 90 10.

Muscadet should be a clean, very dry wine. Even more dry is the second wine of the region, the Gros Plant du Pays Nantais, which often has an aggressive acidity. Both wines go well with the local shellfish.

Some red wine is also made, generally from the Gamay grape. The best is the Coteaux d'Ancenis, which resembles a simple fruity Beaujolais.

The Château de Goulaine

The road from Nantes out to the centre of the vineyards is the N149. Just 11km (7 miles) from the centre of Nantes, on the left-hand side, is the Château de Goulaine, which has been in the same family for more than a thousand years. While it may be more impressive than most, this is typical of many of the châteaux of the region, working country-houses rather than flamboyant palaces. This is the charm of the Muscadet; it is a gentle region with good food and

The town of Ancenis lies on the north bank of the River Loire, between the vineyards of Muscadet and Anjou. Close to the Château lies the Co-operative cellar.

warm hospitality. The narrow valleys of the Sèvre and the Maine gives patches of woodland among the vineyards.

Clisson

While Vallet may claim to be the capital of the Muscadet, the town of Clisson makes a good centre and is rather prettier. Most of the town was destroyed at the end of the 18th century and it was largely rebuilt, in the Italian style, by Cacault, who had been the French ambassador in Rome. There is also an impressive castle standing on a rock, on the left bank of the Sèvre.

For the driver with time only for the Loire Valley, Ancenis is the place to gain a glimpse of the vineyards of Muscadet.

Cognac

Cognac is one of the greatest spirits in the world. It is a brandy, the distillation of wine, and as there are many whiskies, so are there many brandies, but only two of them, Cognac and Armagnac, have reputations based firmly on the source of their wines and the method of distillation.

The fertile chalky countryside around the town of Cognac, on the river Charente, gives thin, acid wines with a low alcoholic degree. It is such wines that give the finest brandies and since distillation began in the region at the beginning of the 15th century it has built up for itself a proud reputation for quality.

The nature of the product lends itself to brand promotion and there are a few companies that dominate world markets. They may not, however, actually own vineyards, or even distil the Cognacs they sell, so there is a broad range of places for the interested tourist to visit.

There are four basic factors that go into the production of a Cognac: the soil, the grapes, the distillation and the ageing.

The area within which Cognac may be produced is quite large, most of the two *départements* of the Charentes. There are vineyards on the Ile de Ré and the Ile d'Oléron in the Atlantic; on the north bank of the Gironde estuary; and around the three towns in the heart of the region, Cognac itself, Jarnac and Saintes. In each of these areas, different soils produce different qualities of wine, giving different qualities of spirit.

For example, a Cognac from the sandy soil of the Ile de Ré may even have a hint of iodine in its flavour from its proximity to the sea. A Cognac from the chalky soil to the south of Cognac itself will have the most finesse and bouquet.

Because of these factors, there is an elaborate hierarchy within the vineyard areas, and the price of the resultant spirit will vary considerably. The finest region is the Grande Champagne to the south of Cognac, then the Petite Champagne, and through the Borderies, Fins Bois, Bons Bois and the fringe Bois Ordinaires and Bois à Terroir.

You can find a Cognac labelled Grande Champagne, which means that it has been distilled solely from wines from that region. A Fine Champagne will be a blend of Grande and Petite Champagne. Most Cognacs, however, will be a blend created to a standard by the various companies from several regions.

Production

The grape varieties grown are mainly the Saint-Emilion, the Colombard and the Folle Blanche, which are often picked before they are fully ripe to ensure sufficient acidity.

Distillation takes place as soon as the wine has finished fermenting, during the winter. It takes place in a copper pot still and there is a double distillation to ensure that the spirit is as pure as possible.

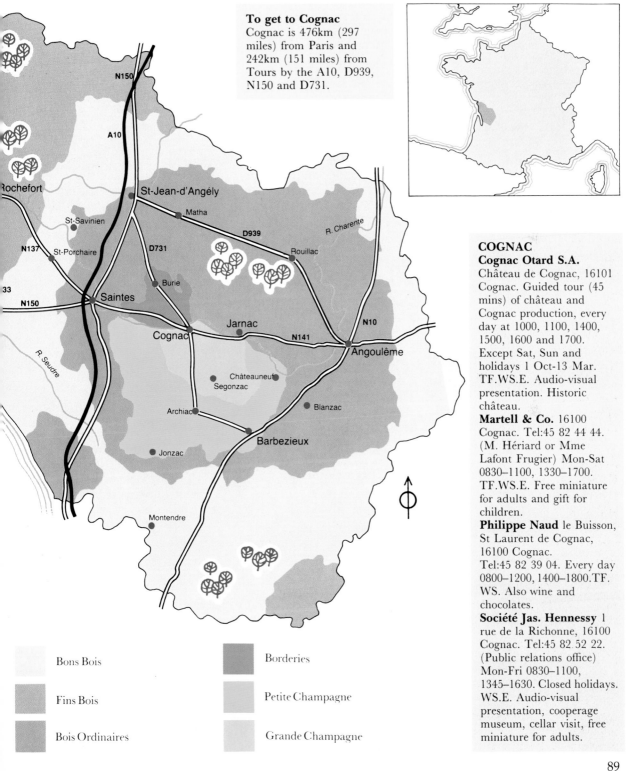

To get to Cognac
Cognac is 476km (297 miles) from Paris and 242km (151 miles) from Tours by the A10, D939, N150 and D731.

COGNAC
Cognac Otard S.A.
Château de Cognac, 16101 Cognac. Guided tour (45 mins) of château and Cognac production, every day at 1000, 1100, 1400, 1500, 1600 and 1700. Except Sat, Sun and holidays 1 Oct-13 Mar. TF.WS.E. Audio-visual presentation. Historic château.
Martell & Co. 16100 Cognac. Tel:45 82 44 44. (M. Hériard or Mme Lafont Frugier) Mon-Sat 0830–1100, 1330–1700. TF.WS.E. Free miniature for adults and gift for children.
Philippe Naud le Buisson, St Laurent de Cognac, 16100 Cognac.
Tel:45 82 39 04. Every day 0800–1200, 1400–1800.TF. WS. Also wine and chocolates.
Société Jas. Hennessy 1 rue de la Richonne, 16100 Cognac. Tel:45 82.52 22. (Public relations office) Mon-Fri 0830–1100, 1345–1630. Closed holidays. WS.E. Audio-visual presentation, cooperage museum, cellar visit, free miniature for adults.

Bons Bois		Borderies	
Fins Bois		Petite Champagne	
Bois Ordinaires		Grande Champagne	

JARNAC
Courvoisier S.A 16200 Jarnac. Tel:45 35 55 55. (Denise Charron) Every day 0930–1130, 1400–1645. Closed Sun May-Oct. WS.E. Wine museum, Napoleonic museum, audio-visual presentation, wine implements, cellars and bottling hall.

ROUILLAC
Claude Audebert les Villairs, 16170 Rouillac. Tel:45 21 76 86. 'We never close.' TF.WS.

ST-JEAN-D'ANGELY
Cognac Bouron Château de la Grange, 17416 St-Jean-d'Angély. Tel:46 32 00 12. (Mme Parias) Mon-Sat 1400–1800. TF.WS.E. 15th-century château.

Vines from three different ages in Cognac. On the left, those that have just been planted; in the middle, some that have been planted a year ago; and mature vines, which will give the acid wine that makes the best spirit.

'The angels' share'
The new spirit is harsh and fiery, so it is put to age in casks of local Tronçais or Limousin oak. The length of time that it is allowed to age depends on the individual company.

During this time the spirit mellows and softens: there is heavy evaporation – I have seen one estimate of the equivalent of 20 million bottles each year. This evaporation, locally called 'the angels' share', blackens the roofs of the warehouses and gives a grimy, industrial air to many of the buildings of Cognac.

Labels
On Cognac labels, there can be a bewildering variety of quality symbols such as the familiar 'three-stars' symbol, V.S.O.P. (Very superior old pale) and Napoleon.

There is very little effective control of the age of these blends, though in theory *** means that the youngest spirit in the blend is at least 30 months old, and in a V.S.O.P., four and a half years old. In both cases the bulk of the Cognac will in fact be considerably older.

Most companies will have small stocks of exceptionally old cognacs, which they store in a warehouse called 'paradise'. This spirit may no longer be in casks but in glass carboys.

Pineau des Charentes
There is one other local speciality that should be tasted. This is the Pineau des Charentes, which comes in two forms, white and rosé. This is a fortified wine made by mixing sweet, unfermented grape juice with brandy. Some companies will also age their Pineau for a considerable time to provide a superior quality.

Scenery and historic towns
The Cognac region is pleasant and varied. It is not a region of intensive viticulture: it is just as renowned, though perhaps in different circles, for its dairy products.

There are beautiful beaches at Royan and on the Ile d'Oléron. You can hire a boat on the languid River Charente: until recently the brandy-boats used to come up it to the little port of Tonnay-Charente to load.

There are also a number of beautiful historic towns. In Cognac, the 10th-century castle now belongs to the Otard company, but it was in the hands of the English for many years, after Richard the Lionheart married his bastard son Philip to Amélie of Cognac. Later the castle was rebuilt by Guy de Lusignan, the son of the widow of King John. Like many of the other important companies in the region, Otard was founded by a British family: the Martells were from the Channel Islands; the Hines from Dorset; and the Hennessys and the Exshaws from Ireland.

Saintes

Historically, the capital of the region was Saintes, some 26km (16 miles) to the west. This was an important Roman town and there are still a number of remains, including an amphitheatre and a triumphal arch. While not a great deal of the former remains, you can still see where the wild beasts were caged.

The arch originally stood on the Roman bridge over the Charente. It was erected during the reign of Nero by Caius Julius Rufus to the memory of Germanicus, Tiberius and Drusus.

In 1844, it was dismantled and re-erected where it now stands.

Just off the N137 which leads north-west out of Saintes is the beautiful Château de la Roche-Courbon, near Saint-Porchaire.

Jonzac, too, has a beautiful 15th-century castle.

In the north-west corner of the Cognac region the pretty port of La Rochelle should be visited. Here the inner harbour is protected by the twin towers of La Chaine and Saint-Nicolas. Finally, in the extreme east of the area is the important town of Angoulême, with its impressive girdle of fortifications.

ST MEME LES CARRIERES
Sté J.P.Ménard et Fils
16720 St Meme les Carrières. Tel:45 81 90 26. (M. Ménard) Mon-Fri 0800–1200, 1400–1800. TF.WS.E. Cellar visit.

FOR FURTHER INFORMATION
Cognac
B.N.I.C. 3 allée de la Corderie, 16100 Cognac. Tel:45 82 66 70.
Pineau des Charentes
Comité National du Pineau des Charentes, 112 ave Victor Hugo, 16100 Cognac. Tel:45 32 09 27.

Copper stills in Cognac. In Cognac, the spirit is distilled twice in these traditional 'pot' stills.

Bordeaux

There are many reasons why the wines of Bordeaux have been the favourite French wines among English-speaking people. First of all, the province of Aquitaine belonged to the English Crown for more than three hundred years.

Secondly, the situation of Bordeaux as a port has made it ideal for the shipment of wine to Britain and the United States. Even during the German occupation in World War II, the gesture that the local resistance fighters made in order to secure more arms from Britain was to load a few casks of their best wine on to a boat and sail for England. Another reason can be seen in the names within the trade. Among the merchants there are Lawtons and Bartons, and the vineyard names include such as Cantenac-Brown, Clarke and Boyd. These are good historical reasons for our interest.

Representatives of the various confréries, *or drinking brotherhoods, of Bordeaux. Each region has its own association, with its individual robes and ceremonies.*

The vineyards of Bordeaux cover a vast area along both banks of the Gironde, and of the two rivers whose estuary this is: the Dordogne and the Garonne. Within this area is a broad range of styles of wine, ranging from the classic red wines of the Haut-Médoc, based on the Cabernet Sauvignon grape, and of Saint-Emilion, on the Merlot, to the dry white wines of the Graves and the luscious sweet wines of Sauternes. However, the great wines with famous names form only a minute proportion of the total production. It has been claimed that there are over three thousand château names in Bordeaux, but of these only a handful are known to even the most devoted wine lover.

The meaning of *château*

It must be pointed out that in Bordeaux the word 'château' may be used in one of its two generally accepted senses – a castle or an imposing country house. However, here the word may also be used to mean anything from the most impressive of palaces to a country cottage, or even a barn. There may not even be a building. The word has come to be synonymous with a vineyard, and not necessarily a distinct vineyard at that, for now many properties sell their second wine under a separate château name. Bordeaux, then, is not just Margaux, Yquem and Cheval Blanc. They may be the apex of the pyramid, but there is a solid base of lesser wines that probably never appear under individual vineyard names.

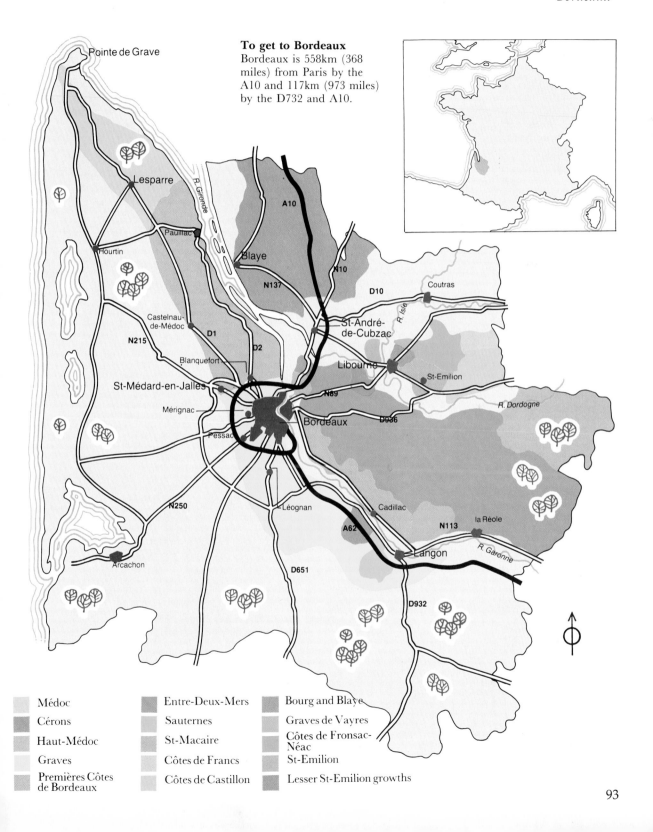

To get to Bordeaux
Bordeaux is 558km (368
miles) from Paris by the
A10 and 117km (973 miles)
by the D732 and A10.

Pointe de Grave

Lesparre

R. Gironde

Pauillac

Hourtin

Blaye

A10

N10

Castelnau-
de-Médoc

N137

N215

D1

D2

Coutras

D10

R. Isle

St-André-
de-Cubzac

Blanquefort

Libourne

St-Médard-en-Jalles

St-Emilion

Mérignac

N89

Bordeaux

R. Dordogne

Pessac

D936

Léognan

Cadillac

N250

la Réole

N113

Arcachon

A62

Langon

R. Garonne

D651

D932

Médoc

Entre-Deux-Mers

Bourg and Blaye

Cérons

Sauternes

Graves de Vayres

Haut-Médoc

St-Macaire

Côtes de Fronsac-
Néac

Graves

Côtes de Francs

St-Emilion

Premières Côtes
de Bordeaux

Côtes de Castillon

Lesser St-Emilion growths

The City of Bordeaux

The waterfront at Bordeaux, which has been described as the most splendid in Europe. Today, fewer boats moor against the historic quays, but Bordeaux is still a thriving city.

Coming into Bordeaux from the north, across the Pont de Pierre, the city unfolds in a vast semi-circle to the right, presenting one of the most attractive waterfronts anywhere in the world. Many of the finest buildings, surrounding the Place de la Bourse, were built in the middle of the 18th century. Further to the right is the Esplanade des Quinconces and further still, the Quai des Chartrons, the former centre of the Bordeaux wine trade.

It was on the waterfront here that the wealthy merchants had their warehouses, on the quays from which ships sailed all over the world. With the coming of long-distance lorries and container-ports, little wine leaves Bordeaux by boat and the *quais* are atrophying.

The warehouses

Most of the merchants have moved to purpose-built, temperature-controlled warehouses outside the city. Only a few retain their token presence on the Chartrons.

In their day, these warehouses, too, were custom-built, running back in narrow strips for a quarter of a mile or more behind the offices at the front. They were cool, for their walls were thick and the barrels could be rolled along the narrow railways provided. The office boy would often ride from one end of the cellar to the other on a bicycle.

There are a few remains from the time when Bordeaux was a Roman city, but the Tour des Anglais bears witness to the time of English occupation.

Graves

The vineyards of Graves come right to the door of Bordeaux. Many have disappeared in the face of rising land prices, but there are still four notable vineyards, even within the motorway corset that now restricts Bordeaux on the southern side.

Of these the most famous is Château Haut-Brion, which can be reached by taking the N250 road in the direction of Arcachon, from the centre of the city. Haut-Brion was classified in 1855 as a *premier grand cru*; the only vineyard from outside the Haut-Médoc to be so honoured.

FOR FURTHER INFORMATION
C.I.V.B. 1 cours du XXX Juillet, 33000 Bordeaux. Tel:56 52 82 82. They have a list of all châteaux welcoming visitors.

In 1787, Thomas Jefferson tried to buy a hogshead of the famous 1784 vintage, through the local honorary American consul, but was refused. He ultimately managed to buy a few cases of 'Obrion', which he shared with a friend. In 1934, the then owner offered the vineyard to the city of Bordeaux, but the gesture was rejected and it was bought by the American banking family, the Dillons, in whose hands it has since remained.

The other châteaux close to the city are La Mission Haut-Brion, La Tour Haut-Brion and, in neighbouring Pessac, Pape-Clément. All these vineyards are particularly known for their red wines, and this is true of all the vineyards of that northern part of the Graves, closest to Bordeaux. Here two new sub-appellations have been created, Graves Pessac and Graves-Léognan.

Léognan

For the amateur with just a little time to spend in Bordeaux, Léognan on the D651 may be the place to visit. Here are such well-known châteaux as Olivier, Haut-Bailly and Domaine de Chevalier.

LEOGNAN
Domain de Chevalier
33850 Léognan. Tel: 56 21 75 27. (M. Bernard or M. Ricard) Mon–Fri 0900–1200,1400–1800 Sat 0900–1200. TF.E.

PESSAC
Château Pape-Clément
216 ave du Dr Nancel Pénard, 33600 Pessac. Tel:56 07 04 11. (M. Musyt or M. Pujol) Mon–Fri 0900–1200,1400–1700. Closed Aug. TF.WS.E. Cellars.

The Haut-Médoc

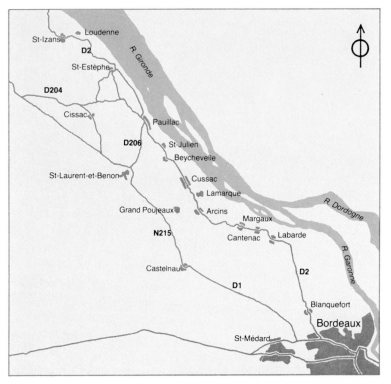

I suppose that the Haut-Médoc is the image of Bordeaux that most of us have in mind: noble châteaux fronted by broad sweeps of gravel and then the vines. It is the most famous region because it is from here that the best wines come – not always the most expensive, for Château Pétrus in Pomerol now seems to have that distinction – but the best red wines.

One of the problems with visiting the Médoc is that it is a long narrow vineyard and that there have not been many reasonable hotels in the area. It is difficult to do it justice in a day, so, unless you are lucky enough to stay in a château, the choice is between a rough and ready rural hotel and a drive back to Bordeaux.

Alternative routes
There are two roads through the Médoc. One is the D2, which winds through the succession of wine villages and seems designed to drop you almost at the front door of every château. The other is a peculiar, but much faster, road, which starts life as the N215, becomes the D1 and then turns back into the N215 once again. This passes to the west of the vineyards, but there are a series of connecting cross-roads to the D2 so you can drive as far as you want up the one and then return by the other.

For this trip, I suggest that you take the D2, which means leaving Bordeaux by the N215 and turning right on the outskirts of the city. The boundary between the Graves and the Haut-Médoc is crossed almost immediately, with the stream called the Jalle de Blanquefort.

The first classified growth, Château La Lagune, comes on the right-hand side and this is shortly

Famous American wine writer Alexis Lichine in front of his grand cru vineyard, Château Prieuré-Lichine, at Margaux.

followed on the left by another, Château Cantemerle.

One thing to note is that the château may not be next to its vineyards; these may be spread out in several blocks in the neighbourhood. Many châteaux, too, have much of their estate in meadows, woodland or garden. You can be certain, though, that if the land is capable of giving good wine, it will be planted.

Margaux

With the hamlets of Labarde and Cantenac, you arrive in the area entitled to call itself Margaux, and it is here that the châteaux begin to come thick and fast. Between the two hamlets, you also cross the railway line that leads all the way up the Médoc from Bordeaux to Pointe de Grave, from where there is a ferry across the Gironde to Royan.

The current Château Margaux was built in a classical style at the beginning of the last century. On the same site there had been a fortress, where Edward III of England had lived. Though classified as a first growth in 1855, the wines went through a bad period and it is only recently, under the direction of Mme Mentzelopoulos, that it has climbed back into the first rank.

After the cluster of classified growths at Margaux, there is something of a lull on the D2. At Arcins, there is an important co-operative cellar for wines from the Haut-Médoc and one can turn left to see the group of châteaux, with the appellation of Moulis, around the village of Grand Poujeaux.

Back on the D2, you come to the village of Lamarque. Parts of its château date back to the 11th century, though most of the present structure is from the 14th. To continue the royal English tradition, it was occupied by Henry V.

Beyond Cussac, the most concentrated group of fine vineyards in the world begins at Beychevelle.

MARGAUX
Château d'Angludet
33460 Cantenac. Tel:56 88 71 41. (Mme Chauvet or Mme Sichel) Mon-Fri 0900–1200, 1400–1700. TF.E.
Château Lascombes
33460 Margaux. Tel:56 88 70 66. (M. Vannetelle) Mon-Fri 0900–1200,1400–1800 (Fri 1700) TF.WS.E.
Château Margaux 33460 Margaux. Tel:56 88 70 28. (Mme Garric) By appointment only. Closed Aug and during vintage. E.
Château Prieuré-Lichine
33460 Cantenac. Tel:56 88 36 28. Every day 0900–1800. TP.WS.E. Collection of firebacks.

CASTELNAU EN MEDOC
Château Chasse-Spleen
Moulis en Médoc, 33480 Castelnau en Médoc. Tel:56 58 02 37. Mon-Fri 0900–1230, 1400–1730. Closed Aug. E. Underground cellars.

LAMARQUE
Ste Civile Gromand d'Evry
Château de Lamarque, 33460 Lamarque. Tel:56 58 90 03 or 56 58 97 55. (Mme Coulary) Mon-Fri 0900–1200, 1400–1730. TP.WS. Old fortress.

Château Beychevelle

This château used to belong to the French high admiral, and as a token of respect all the boats sailing past on the Gironde used to lower their sails (*baisse-voile*). This became corrupted to the present name.

Off to the left is Château Lagrange, which though classified in 1855, had fallen on hard times until it was purchased (in December 1983) by the Japanese whisky group, Suntory. They have already spent more than 150 million francs in restoring the vineyards, the press-house and cellars and the château.

Pauillac

Châteaux Lagrange and Beychevelle have the appellation Saint-Julien – one that they share with many of the finest wines of Bordeaux, though none of them are classified as first growths. The town of Pauillac though, has three first growths: Mouton-Rothschild, Latour and Lafite-Rothschild.

In the 1855 classification, Mouton was only rated as a second growth. For more than a century it was in a rather ambivalent position, for it considered itself to be a first growth in all but name. In a bid to strengthen its position it used to charge as much as, and sometimes

more than, the first growths. This led to an unfortunate leapfrogging situation and a price-spiral. In fact it took a ministerial decree, in 1973, to confirm its status as a *premier cru*.

Among the owners of Château Latour are the Bristol wine merchants John Harvey and the owners of the *Financial Times*, the Pearson group. The vineyard takes its name from a 19th-century tower standing by the château, which is reputed to have been built of stone from a fort that previously stood on the site.

Château Lafite-Rothschild is a showplace that opens its gates very rarely to visitors. It is a beautiful château standing in a beautiful park. It stands on the northern boundaries of Pauillac and is almost overshadowed by a Shell petrol refinery. Beyond lies the last of the village appellations of the Haut-Médoc, Saint-Estèphe.

Saint-Estèphe

While Pauillac may give the fullest wines, Margaux the most delicate, and Saint-Julien the richest, those of Saint-Estèphe have the tendency to be the most austere, they take some time to soften out and become great wines.

Perhaps the best-known wine of the village is Château Cos d'Estournel, which has a striking position on a small hill on the right-hand side of the road. Striking the architecture certainly is, for there is no other château quite like this in all Bordeaux. To build one's cow-sheds in the form of an oriental folly must have taken some imagination – and a lot of money. This is exactly what Louis Gaspard d'Estournelle, the then owner, did 170 years ago.

ST-JULIEN
Château Beychevelle
33250 St-Julien Beychevelle. Tel:56 59 23 00. (Mme Lauzy) Mon-Fri 0930–1200,1400–1730. WS.E.
Château Lagrange 33250 St Julien Beychevelle. Tel:56 59 23 63. (Mlle Catherine Munck) Mon-Fri 0900–1100,1400–1600. Closed Aug. TF.WS.E.

CISSAC
Château Cissac 33250 Cissac. Tel:56 59 58 13. Mon-Fri 0900–1130, 1430–1630. TF.WS.E. Possibility of tasting wines from a variety of châteaux.
Château Hanteillan 33250 Cissac. Tel:56 59 35 31. Mon-Sat 0800–1200, 1400–1800. TF.WS.E. Collection of Greek and Roman wine-related objects.
S.C.Château Lamothe 33250 Cissac. Tel:56 59 58 16. (M. Fabre) Mon-Fri 0900–1130, 1430–1730. TF.WS.E. Picnic area.

PAUILLAC
Château Lafite-Rothschild 33250 Pauillac. Tel:56 59 01 74. By appointment only: telephone Paris (1) 42 56 33 50, and confirm in writing at least 10 days before arrival. Mon-Fri 0900–1200,1500–1800. Closed 15 Sep-15 Nov. TF.WS.E.
Château Lynch-Bages 33250 Pauillac. Tel:56 59 25 59. (M. Llose) Mon-Fri 0900–1130,1400–1700. Closed 2nd half of Aug. TF.E.

Château Mouton-Rothschild 33250 Pauillac. Tel:56 59 22 22. (Mlle Courtiade) By appointment only. Mon-Fri 0930–1200,1400–1700 (Fri 1600)

Château Pichon Longueville Baron 33250 Pauillac. Tel:56.59.00.82. (M. Matignon) Mon-Fri 0900–11.30,1400–1700. Closed 2nd half of Aug. TF.E.

Château Pichon Longueville Comtesse de Lalande 33250 Pauillac. Tel:56.59.19.40. Mon-Fri 0900–1200,1400–1600. TF.WS.E. Terrace with view over vineyards and Gironde.

ST-ESTEPHE
Château Cos d'Estournel 33250 St-Estèphe. Tel:56 44 11 37. Mon-Fri 0900–1200,1500–1700. TP.WS.E. Audio-visual presentation.

FOR FURTHER INFORMATION
Conseil des Vins du Médoc 1 cours du 30 Juillet, 33000 Bordeaux. Tel:56 48 18 62.
Maison du Médoc place du Tribunal, 33340 Lesparre. Tel:56 41 85 65.
Maison du Tourisme et du Vin de Médoc quai Léon Perrier, 33250 Pauillac. Tel:56 59 03 08.
Maison du Vin de Margaux place la Trémoille, 33460 Margaux. Tel:56 88 70 82.
Maison du Vin de St-Estèphe place de l'Eglise, 33250 St-Estèphe. Tel:56 59 30 59.

If you turn left, just beyond Cos d'Estournel, you come to the small village of Cissac. While it has no classified growths in the 1855 table, there is little doubt that when a new table comes to be created it will have some candidates for the lower ranks.

The Haut-Médoc finishes at the northern boundary of Saint-Estèphe. To the north, the wines only have right to the appellation Médoc.

The tower which gives its name to Château Latour at Pauillac, which many experts say produces the finest wine in Bordeaux.

Many of these are very sound wines. One vineyard that is of particular note is Château Loudenne, which was set up as a model estate during the last century by the Gilbey family. The property even had its own quay, so that the wine could be shipped direct to Britain.

The White Wines of Bordeaux

In the 18th century, the property belonged to the Benedictine monks of Sainte-Croix, and they were the first to plant white grapes. The story has it that a beautiful young girl from the region was captured by the Sultan of Constantinople and she introduced him to the wine, which, because of his religious principles, she called Carbonnieux Mineral Water. He became one of the monks' most regular customers!

A few kilometres further along at Labrède is the beautiful château, surrounded by a moat, where Montesquieu was born. This was rebuilt in 1429 on what remained of an earlier fortress.

At the village of Podensac there is, by the side of the main road, the Maison des Vins de Graves, open

In every town, and most villages in France, the weekly market plays an important part in shopping.

It was not very long ago that the white wines of Bordeaux were not being treated very seriously, but now all that has changed. The great sweet white wines have come back into fashion and modern wine-making techniques, and the Sauvignon grape, have created a new generation of crisp white wines. In the past, few of the wines could truly have been described as dry, but this is no longer the case.

There is some white wine made in most of the Bordeaux regions – even Château Margaux produces a little called Pavillon Blanc de Château Margaux – but the finest are produced upstream from Bordeaux on both banks of the Garonne.

The vineyards of the Graves close to Bordeaux are best known for their red wines, but as you drive south-west, parallel to the motorway on the N113, you move steadily into white wine country.

Château Carbonnieux, at Léognan, in fact produces slightly more red wine than white, but there is an amusing story about the latter.

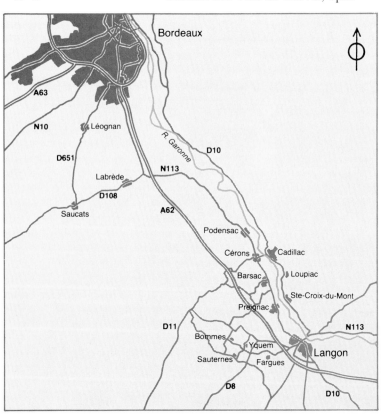

every day in July, August and September, where information about the local wines can be obtained. Podensac is also the beginning of the area producing sweet white wines with the appellation Cérons.

Here the situation is slightly confused, for the local growers have the choice of making a dry white wine or a red wine that they can call Graves, or a sweet white wine called Cérons. At the moment, about four times as much dry wine is produced in the village as sweet.

Sweet white wines

To make a great sweet wine in Bordeaux is not an easy, or a cheap, process. It is achieved by picking the grapes late in the autumn, when they have been attacked by what is known as the noble rot, *Botrytis cinerea*. This feeds on the water in the grapes, but leaves the sugar. The resulting grape is shrivelled like a raisin but extremely sweet. Naturally, the yields are very low, for there is little juice in the grapes. The noble rot is encouraged by

autumn mists and thus the greatest vineyards making this type of wine are nearly always close to water; in this case the Garonne.

At vintage time, the pickers will pass through the vineyards three or four times, just picking those grapes that have been affected by the rot.

There are three reasons, therefore, for the high cost of these wines: perfect, long warm autumns are needed, yields are very low, and the vintages are labour intensive.

Sauternes

The finest of these sweet wines are called Sauternes and they come from the vineyards of five small villages on the right of the main road. The first of these is Sauternes itself (from which comes the noble, and expensive, Château d'Yquem), Bommes, Fargues, Preignac and Barsac.

The wines from this last village can call themselves Barsac, rather than Sauternes. Barsac wines are generally considered to have rather less intense sweetness than the normal Sauternes, but rather more finesse.

LEOGNAN
Château Carbonnieux
33850 Léognan. Tel:56 87 08 28. (Eric Perrin) Mon-Fri 0800–1200,1400–1800. WS.E.

PORTETS
Château Rahoul 33640 Portets. Tel:57 67 01 12. (Mme Court) By appointment only. Mon-Fri WS.E.

The beautiful Château de Labrède in the Graves, built in the 15th century and the birthplace of Montesquieu.

LANGON
Château Filhot Sauternes, 33210 Langon. Tel:56 63 61 09. (Henri de Vaucelles) Every day 0900–1900.TF (with purchase) WS.E.

PREIGNAC
Château Gilette 33210 Preignac. Tel:56 63 27 59. (Christian and Mme Medeville) Mon-Fri 0830–1200, 1400–1800. Closed Aug. TF.WS.

FOR FURTHER INFORMATION
Graves Syndicat Viticole des Graves et des Graves Superieurs, 3 rue François Mauriac, 33720 Podensac. Tel:56 27 09 25.
The sweet white wines
Maison du Vin de Sauternes, place de la Mairie, Sauternes, 33210 Langon. Tel:56 63 60 37. Maison du Vin de Cadillac, Château des Ducs d'Epernon, 33410 Cadillac. Tel:56 27 31 08.

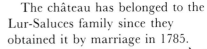

Sauternes – the grapes

Three varieties of grape are used in the manufacture of Sauternes: the Semillon, normally about three-quarters of the whole; the Sauvignon, about a quarter; and traces of the Muscadelle.

Château d'Yquem

While everybody has their favourite Sauternes, it is generally considered that the finest is made at Château d'Yquem. As with the wines of the Haut-Médoc, those of the Sauternes were classified in 1855, and this was the only one to be rated *Premier Cru Superieur*.

The château has belonged to the Lur-Saluces family since they obtained it by marriage in 1785.

In poor years no wine will be sold as Château d'Yquem, but in some years a dry white wine is made called 'Y' (pronounced *ygrec*). This is produced from 50 per cent Sauvignon grapes and 50 per cent Semillon – at Yquem there is no Muscadelle planted.

Other great Sauternes

There are a number of other great wines made including Coutet and Climens from Barsac; Rieussec at Fargues; Suduiraut at Preignac; and Latour-Blanche at Bommes. This last belongs to the French state and is run as a form of wine school for local, and other, growers.

One question is, 'When to drink Sauternes?' The French seem to like to drink it at the beginning of a meal and suggest that it is the ideal accompaniment for foie gras. For most of us that would certainly restrict the consumption! I feel that it is better at the end of a meal – it can go well with nuts or even certain strong cheeses like Roquefort.

Langon

The capital of the white wine district is Langon (an old guide book in front of me describes one hotel as 'dirty, but good food') and here there is an excellent restaurant in Claude Darroze. One can then either return to Bordeaux directly by the motorway, or cross over the Garonne and return via the vineyard areas on the other bank.

A traditional part of the cookery of the Bordeaux region is grilling over a fire of vine-shoots. This gives the meat a distinctive taste. Here, the chef at the Grillebois at Cérons turns the steaks.

Entre Deux Mers

The vast area between the Garonne and Dordogne rivers is known as the Entre Deux Mers, 'between two seas'. It claims to be the largest single *appellation contrôlée* in France. Here, the growers have decided that their future lies in making clean, dry white wines. This red has to be called Bordeaux or Bordeaux Supérieur.

It is a region of rolling countryside with small villages. In the south there are a number of fortified mills. There are also market towns established by the English, like Sauveterre de Guyenne. This is a gentle area off the normal routes.

Premières Côtes de Bordeaux

The D10, along the east bank of the Garonne, is a pretty route between the river and vineyard slopes producing, for the most part, sweet white wine. Much of this is sold as Premières Côtes de Bordeaux. There are, however, three smaller areas, each with a right to its own appellation: Cadillac, Sainte-Croix-du-Mont and Loupiac, sometimes described as 'the poor man's Sauternes'.

For long these wines were out of fashion and the growers were in despair. It is pleasant to see that the tide has turned and they are coming into their own once again.

The finest wine demands the finest cask. A cooper in the Sauternais prepares an oak cask for ageing the local wine.

Bourg and Blaye

Tasting the red wines at Château Tayac at Bourg. Most vineyards welcome visitors, but not many have such well-developed tasting facilities as this.

To the north of Blaye, the vineyards finish, as the land turns into a sandy marsh. Here there is a nuclear power station looking across the river to Saint-Estèphe.

Before the planting of the vineyards in the Médoc, it was those of Bourg and Blaye that made the reputation of the wines of Bordeaux. Now they concentrate on producing light, early-maturing red wines, with a lot of fruit, and clean, dry white wines. Much of the latter is turned into sparkling wine by a large producer outside Bourg.

The countryside is very pretty, much hillier than most of Bordeaux, consisting largely of a series of rolling ridges, running parallel to the river, topped with attractive little châteaux.

For the lover of churches, there are a number in the area that date back to before the time of the English occupation.

There are few who would claim that the vineyards of Bordeaux are beautiful. There are beautiful châteaux and there is some agreeable countryside, but if it were not for the wines, there are few places where one would drive just for the view. One of the exceptions is in the region of Bourg and Blaye.

Bourg is a pleasant town, which for nearly a year during the siege of Bordeaux in the 17th century was the seat of the French court. The road from there leads along the bank of the river at the foot of chalky cliffs. There are wonderful views across the flat islands in the river to the Haut-Médoc and its châteaux.

The town of Blaye is dominated by the citadel which was built by Vauban to command the approaches to the Gironde, together with Fort-Médoc at Cussac, and Fort du Pâté on a small island in the middle of the river. The strategic importance of Blaye had been recognized by the Romans who built a fort there. Gastronomically, it has some importance as it is the centre of a limited caviare industry.

BLAYE
S.A. Bayle Carreau
Château Pardaillan, Cars, 33390 Blaye. Tel:57 64 32 43. Mon-Fri 0830–1200, 1400–1800. TF.WS.E.

FOR FURTHER INFORMATION
Maison du Vin de Blaye et de Bourg allées Marines, 33390 Blaye. Tel:57 42 02 45.

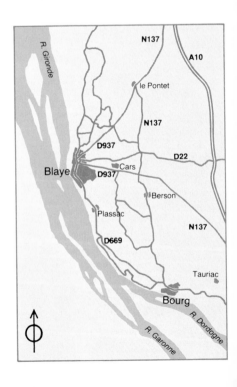

Pomerol

The vineyards of Pomerol form an angled square, with one corner in the centre of the old wine port of Libourne (which is today better known for its excellent food market). Each side of the square measures no more than 3km (2 miles), so the area is small.

There were vineyards here in Roman times and the viticultural tradition was maintained by the Knights of St John of Jerusalem, who built a manor house, a hospital and a church in the neighbourhood.

Château Pétrus

This is an area of small vineyard properties; even the most famous, Château Pétrus, produces no more than 160 casks in an average vintage, less than a sixth of Château Latour, for example.

Here, the Merlot is the dominant grape variety, and it gives a wine that is believed by some to resemble the wines of Burgundy, for it has a rich, velvety taste not found elsewhere in Bordeaux.

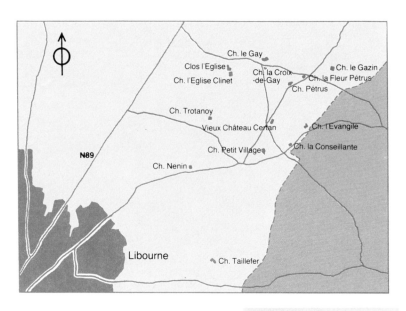

The Pomerol vineyards are split in two by the N89, which follows the route of an old Roman road.

To the west of this road, the soil has a sandy base, and this gives wines that are lighter and rather lacking in character. All the finest wines come from the eastern side of the road, where the gravelly soil gives them much more 'backbone'.

POMEROL
Château la Croix de Gay and **Château la Fleur de Gay** Pomerol, 33500 Libourne. Tel:57 51 19 05. Every day 0900–1200, 1330–1600. TF.WS.E.
Château Petit Village Pomerol, 33500 Libourne. Tel:56 44 11 37. (M. Bruno Prats) By appointment only.

Château Loumède in the Blayais is typical of many of the properties in Bordeaux, with a variety of architectural styles developed over the centuries.

Saint-Emilion

If I were asked to nominate the three most complete wine towns in France, they would be Beaune, in Burgundy; Riquewihr, in Alsace; and Saint-Emilion. Coincidentally, each of them has a compactness given by town walls. Perhaps it is these that have helped to preserve, and concentrate, the character in each case.

A town rich in history

Much of Saint-Emilion's history is recalled in the names of many of the châteaux. The vineyards were first planted by the Romans, and the poet Ausonius (who also appreciated the wines of the Moselle) is supposed to have found his wife in Bordeaux and to have lived in Saint-Emilion. His name is remembered in the great wines of Château Ausone.

For a time the region was occupied by the Moors (Château Villemaurine) and then became an important ecclesiastical centre, as is borne out by such names as Château le Couvent, which is actually within the town walls, Clos la Madeleine and Clos de l'Oratoire.

It is not easy to decide what to advise the visitor to see in the town. There are the underground church and the catacombs, the Couvent des Jacobins, the Collegiate Church, with its beautiful cloisters, the town walls and the cave retreat of the 8th-century St Aemilianus, who gave his name to the town. For the person who wants to have the decision taken out of his hands, regular guided tours on foot leave the tourist office in the Place des Créneaux during the summer months.

The appellation Saint-Emilion includes a host of châteaux, with vineyards, in eight communes, on

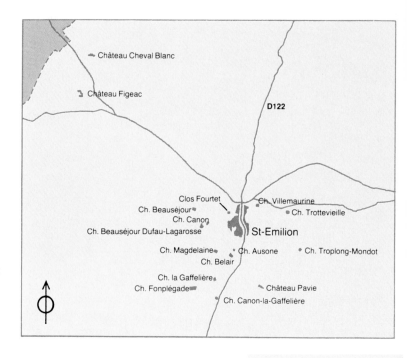

three distinct types of soil, and, therefore, of three distinct qualities. Perhaps surprisingly, the final decision as to which villages could call their wine Saint-Emilion came as late as 1929, and was based on rights granted in 1289.

The first of the vineyard types is the continuation of the plateau with its chalky soil, rich in iron, of the vineyards of Pomerol. Here the two outstanding châteaux are Cheval Blanc and Figeac.

Around the town itself, the plateau falls away to the plain. On the slopes, where the soil is similar, are the vineyards of the Côtes, with ideal exposure to the south-east. Here, the château with the highest reputation is Ausone, followed by Belair, Pavie and la Gaffelière.

Down on the plain, where the soil is a mixture of sand and gravel, the quality of the wine can be distinctly inferior, yet it still benefits from the name Saint-Emilion. Perhaps

ST-EMILION
Dubois-Challon Château Belair, 33300 St-Emilion. Tel:57 24 70 94. (M. Delbeck) By appointment only. 1100–1900. TF.WS.E. Historic cellars.
Consorts Valette Château Pavie, 33300 St-Emilion. Tel:57 24 72 02. Mon-Fri 0930–1200,1430–1700. TF.E. Cellars dug into the rock.
Château Villemaurine 33240 St-Emilion, Tel:57 74 46 44. (Mlle Bernadette Musset) Tue-Sat 0800–1200, 1400–1800. TP.WS.E.

FRONSAC
Château de la Riviére St-Michel de Fronsac, 33126 Fronsac. Tel:57 24 98 01. Mon-Fri 0800–1100, 1400–1700. TP (money reimbursed with purchase of 6 bottles) WS.E.

because of this weakness, there has developed an immensely complicated system of classification. The two top classifications are Saint-Emilion *Premier Grand Cru Classé* and Saint-Emilion *Grand Cru Classé*. These are re-assessed every ten years. At the moment, there are 11 in the first category – though two of them, Ausone and Cheval Blanc, are given a higher rating within the category – and about 70 in the second.

In addition, each year, any vineyard can send its wine to be sampled and, if it is found worthy, it is given the status of *Grand Cru* for that particular vintage. In any given year, there might be hundreds of such wines. This means that the honour of just about every grower in the area is satisfied.

Most Saint-Emilion is made from the Merlot and Cabernet Franc grapes. At its best it is one of the most satisfying wines of Bordeaux, having a rich fruitiness which appeals to those put off by the austerity of many of the wines of the Médoc.

Surrounding the vineyards of Pomerol and Saint-Emilion, there are a number of areas producing similar wines. Indeed, before the coming of *appellation contrôlée*, much of their wine used to be sold under their names, and some of these areas have since gained reflected glory by adding one or the other name to their own. These areas include Lalande de Pomerol, Lussac-Saint-Emilion, Saint-Georges-Saint-Emilion, Puisseguin-Saint-Emilion, Fronsac and Côtes de Castillon.

FOR FURTHER INFORMATION
Syndicat Viticole et Agricole de St-Emilion B.P.15, 33330 St-Emilion. Tel:57 24 72 17.
Maison du Vin de St-Emilion place Pierre-Meyrat, 33330 St-Emilion. Tel:57 74 42 42.
Syndicat Viticole de Fronsac Plaisance, 33126 Fronsac. Tel:57 51 80 51.

The historic town of St-Emilion, with its vineyards even breaking through its walls. To the left is the Norman-style castle, built by Louis VIII.

Bergerac and Cahors

BERGERAC
Domaine de Haut-Pecharmant 24100 Bergerac. Tel:53 57 29 50. (Michel Roches or Françoise Lagrange) Every day 0800– 1200, 1400–1930. TF.WS.E. Picnic area.

Château de Monbazillac
Monbazillac, 24240 Sigoulès. Tel:53 57 06 38. (Mme Bortot) June-Sep, every day 0930–1230, 1400–1930. Oct-May 0900–1200, 1400–1800. TP including visit to château.

FOR FURTHER INFORMATION
Bergerac
C.I.V.R.B. 2 place du Dr. Cayla, 24100 Bergerac. Tel:53 57 12 57.
Cahors
Syndicat Interprofessionel du Vin de Cahors, Chambre d'Agriculture du Lot, ave Jean-Jaurès, 46004 Cahors. Tel:65 22 55 30.

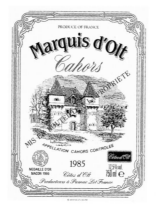

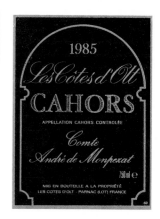

The Chateau of Monbazillac, which now belongs to the local co-operative cellar, and houses a restaurant and museum.

In the Middle Ages, most of the wine that was shipped from Bordeaux came not from the local vineyards, but from what was called the Haut-Pays, up the Dordogne and the Garonne and their tributaries. Today, there are still wines from those regions, with the best probably coming from around Bergerac on the Dordogne and Cahors on the Lot.

The vineyards of Bergerac are a logical continuation of those of Bordeaux and they produce a range of wines that are remarkably similar. The finest dry white wines come from the vineyards of Montravel, on both sides of the main road from Bordeaux and Libourne, to the west of Sainte-Foy-la-Grande.

The finest sweet wines, produced in the same way and from the same grapes as Sauternes, come from around the town of Monbazillac, to the south of Bergerac.

The local red wines are similar to the lighter clarets, with the finest having the appellation Pécharmant.

Cahors

The town of Cahors is built on and around a rock in a sweeping bend in the river Lot. Its most striking feature is the fortified Valentré bridge, built five hundred years ago. It is the centre of the gastronomic region of Quercy, long reputed for its walnuts and its truffles.

The basic grape of Cahors is the Malbec, here called the Auxerrois, which plays a supporting role in Bordeaux. Traditional methods of vinification used to give what was known as a 'black' wine, deep in colour, full of tannin and long-lasting. Modern wine-making methods and more planting in the sandy valley bottom, rather than on the limestone slopes, now give rather lighter, but by no means light, wines which mature earlier.

Armagnac

After Cognac, the second great brandy of France is Armagnac. This comes from a region to the south-east of Bordeaux. As in Cognac, there are distinctive vineyard regions: to the east and south, the hilly Haut-Armagnac; in the middle, centred on Condom, the Ténarèze; and to the west, the sandy-soiled Bas-Armagnac. It is from this last that the best spirits come. In some ways Armagnac might be said to be a country cousin to Cognac and indeed they are related, for some of the more important Armagnac companies belong to Cognac houses.

It is, however, an area of small producers selling an individual product. There appears to be a measure of pragmatism as to the method of distillation, but the traditional Armagnac is still a hybrid between the pot still of Cognac and malt whisky, and the patent still of grain whisky.

Distillation

The spirit is distilled only once and comes off the still at a relatively low strength, thus having in it a higher proportion of congenerics, or flavours. It is then aged in casks made from the local oak, which naturally imparts a great deal of colour and softens the spirit more rapidly than does the wood used for ageing Cognac. Most Armagnac is then put into the distinctive regional bottle, the *gascon*.

Is it better than Cognac? That is a matter of personal taste. It is a bit like saying, 'Is Burgundy better than claret?' Some like one, some like the other, and many like both. Armagnac tends to be more flavoursome and, perhaps, less smooth. It will appeal to the person who is looking for something different after a meal.

There is also a local aperitif, floc de Gascogne, similar to Pineau des Charentes.

CONDOM
Armagnac Janneau 50 ave d'Aquitaine, 32100 Condom. Tel:62 28 24 77. Mon-Fri 0900–1200, 1400–1700. TF.WS.E. Museum.
Armagnac Larressingle Papelorey S.A. rue des Carmes. 32100 Condom. Tel:62 22 15 33. (M. Papelorey) Mon-Fri 0830–1200,1330–1730. Closed 1st fortnight in Aug. TF.WS.E. Cellar visit.

EAUZE
Grassa et Fils Château Tariquet, 32800 Eauze. Tel:62 09 87 82. By appointment only. TF.WS. Armagnac and *vin de pays*.

GONDRIN
Armagnac Veuve Goudoulin Clos du Presbytère, rte de Vic-Fézensac, Courrensan, 32330 Gondrin. Tel:62 06 35 02. (M. Faure) Mon-Fri 0900–1200, 1400–1800. TF.WS.E.

VIC-FEZENSAC
Ets. Gelas et Fils 32190 Vic-Fézensac. Tel:62 06 30 11. (M. Philippe Gelas or Mlle Catherine Zago) Mon-Fri 0900–1200, 1400–1800. TF.WS.E. Armagnac and Eau de Vie from plums.

FOR FURTHER INFORMATION
B.N.I.A Place de la Liberté, 32800 Eauze. Tel:62 09 82 33.

Casks ageing in the cellars of Janneau, to many people the best-known name of Armagnac.

The South-West

In many places in the south-west of France there are small vineyard areas with either *appellation contrôlée* or V.D.Q.S. status striving to better their reputation. In some cases, the move may be led by a single dedicated grower, in others most of the production may be in the hands of a co-operative cellar. In either case, local wine-making might have come to an end but for these efforts.

The region is crossed by two motorways running almost parallel. To the north, there is the A62, then the A61, which joins Bordeaux to Toulouse and the Mediterranean; to the south, the nascent A64 running along the foothills of the Pyrenees. Many of the small vineyard regions lie close to these motorways and could make a short but interesting diversion.

Some 80km (50 miles) from Bordeaux, on the A62, the vineyards of the Côtes du Marmandais lie to the left. Here a variety of Bordeaux and local grapes go to make easy-drinking red wines. More serious are those of the Côtes de Buzet, produced on the south bank of the Garonne in the 30km (20 miles) before Agen. The

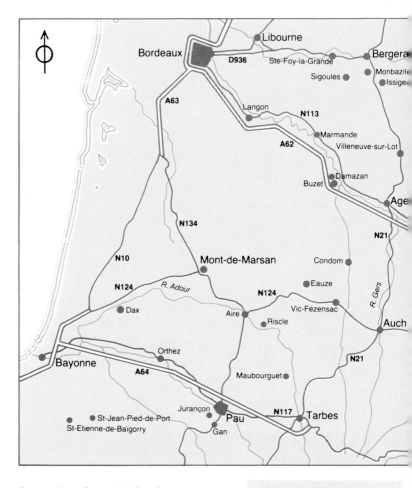

best wines from the local co-operative cellar have shown well against wines from Bordeaux in blind tastings.

On the left of the motorway, before Toulouse, is the small town of Fronton, around which are made fruity red wines with a basis of the Negrette grape. The largest property in the area is the ambitious Château Bellevue la Forêt.

Further to the north-east is the important historical vineyard region of Gaillac. Here are made red, white, rosé and slightly sparkling wines from a very broad range of grape varieties. There is a mixture of qualities, probably depending on the

COTES DE BUZET
Les Vignerons Reunis des Côtes de Buzet Buzet-sur-Baise, 47160 Damazan. Tel:35 84 74 30. Mon-Fri 0900–1200, 1400–1800.

FRONTON
Château Bellevue la Forêt rte D48, 31620 Fronton. Tel:61 82 43 21. Mon-Sat 0830–1200, 1400–1730. TF.WS.E.

GAILLAC
Cave de Labastide Labastide de Lévis, 81150 Marssac. Tel:63 55 41 83. Mon-Fri 0900–1200, 1400–1800. TF.WS.

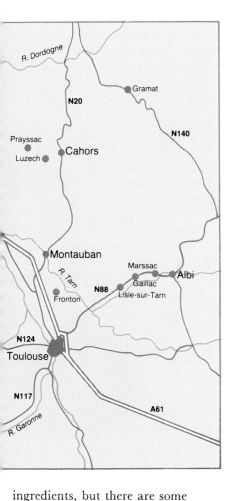

the finest white wine is Jurançon (yet another wine to use the ubiquitous Henri IV in its publicity).

Jurançon used to be a sweet wine, picked late to obtain the maximum amount of sugar in the grapes. Because of the cost involved and the comparatively small demand, however, the sweet variety, capable of ageing many years, is now something of a rarity. More commonly, Jurançon is a steely dry wine.

Irouléguy

Finally from the Basque country, there are the reds and rosés of Irouléguy. Here, around the beautiful town of Saint-Jean-Pied-de-Port only 90 hectares (215 acres) are left in production, with all the wine being made by the local co-operative.

However, ambitious plans by a number of local growers have led to a further 50 hectares being planted on the steep hillsides. Let us hope that their optimism will pay dividends.

GAILLAC
J.H.F.de Faramond
Château de Lastours, 81310 L'Isle-sur-Tarn. Every day 0900–1200, 1400–1800. TF.WS. Historic château.

JURANCON
Caves des Producteurs de Jurançon 53 ave Henri IV, 64290 Gan. Tel:59 21 57 03. Jul-Aug every day 0800–1900 Sep-Jun Mon-Sat 0800–1200, 1400–1900. TF.WS.E.

MADIRAN
Domaine Pichard
Soublecause, 65700 Maubourguet. Tel:62 96 46 76. (M. Vigneau or M. Tachouères) Mon-Fri 0900–1200, 1400–1730. TF.WS.

A peaceful scene in the Basque town of St-Jean-Pied-de-Port, in the foothills of the Pyrennees, not far from the Spanish frontier.

ingredients, but there are some excellent red and rosé wines.

The wine that is drunk most often in the restaurants of the Armagnac region comes from the south. This is Madiran, made largely from the Tannat grape. Rather rough and ready when young, it develops with ageing into an excellent, full-bodied wine. The local white wine is the Pacherenc (a grape variety) de Vic Bilh. This has an intense flavour and is made, according to the vintage, in a variety of degrees of sweetness.

Also made in the area is a little Béarn, in red, white and rosé, though most of it is produced to the south, west of the town of Pau. Here

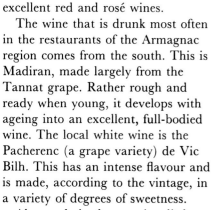

Languedoc-Roussillon

Wine-drinking is on the decline in France in a dramatic fashion. The daily litre of red is no longer a necessity, while the sales of soft drinks and beer are increasing. This does not mean that the sales of all wines are decreasing. On the contrary, the sales of *appellation contrôlée* wines are mounting in France. The plastic litre bottle is being replaced by the 75cl glass bottle.

This change in habits is presenting severe problems to those regions where the ordinary wines were produced, the four *départements* of the Pyrenees-Orientales, Aude, Hérault and Gard, known collectively as Languedoc-Roussillon. While Brussels might offer subsidies for vineyards to be uprooted, that subsidy is worth little if there is no alternative way of making a living. The answer for many is to try to make better wines by planting better grape varieties and by improving vinification techniques. Less, and better, must be their reply.

To get to Languedoc Roussillon
Montpellier is 759km (474 miles) and 101km (63 miles) from Orange by A6, A7 and A9. Narbonne is 850km (531 miles) from Paris by A6, A7 and A9 and 386km (241 miles) from Bordeaux by A62 and A61.

When France had Algeria as a colony, the role of the vineyards of the south was to produce large quantities of thin, light wine to blend with the highly coloured and alcoholic wines of North Africa, to make wines for everyday drinking. High-yielding grape varieties, such as the Aramon, were planted for this purpose.

With the loss of Algeria, and the entry of France into the Common Market, this business was lost overnight – a disaster for this region dedicated solely to wine production. Since then, efforts have been made to rectify the situation by upgrading the many small wines of the region, such as Corbières and Minervois, and by introducing the status of *vin de pays*, a *vin de table* from a specific area with an individual story to tell.

In the forefront of these efforts to raise the status of the local wines have been many of the co-operative cellars, which have been responsible for the bulk of the production. Behind them are an increasing number of individual properties making their own wines with their own personality. It has not been easy, for the growers have had to reduce their yields without being certain that they would sell their wine in the end. There has been much replanting too, with better grape varieties such as the Syrah and the Cabernet Sauvignon. While Languedoc and Roussillon seem generally to be joined, they have separate histories. The province of Roussillon largely corresponded to the *département* of Pyrénées-Orientales, with the city of Perpignan as its centre.

I find Perpignan rather drab, dominated as it is by its historical role as a gateway to France, with the consequent military implications. Over the town stands the Citadel, whose inner walls were built by Charles V and the outer by France's most noted military architect, Vauban. At its centre is the palace of the Kings of Majorca.

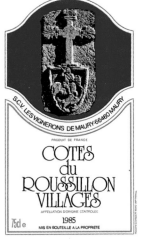

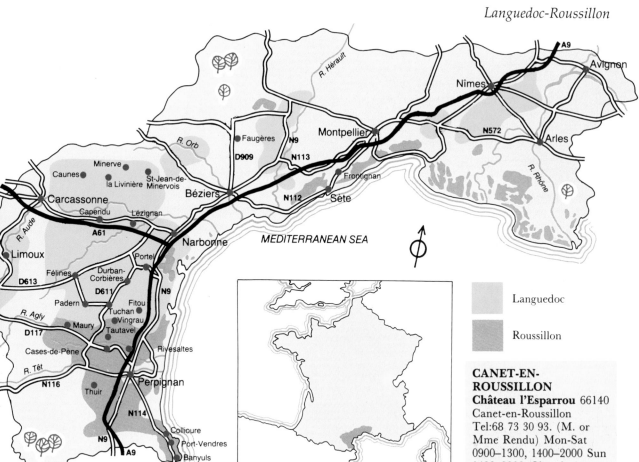

Côtes du Roussillon

To the east of Perpignan, along the Mediterranean beaches, there is a string of resorts, with behind them the vineyards of Côtes du Roussillon. Inland, to the south-west, is the town of Thuir, a centre for the production of flavoured aperitif wines.

The best wines of the area, which have the right to the appellation Côtes du Roussillon-Villages, come from north of the city.

If you leave by the D117, past the airport, you will pass the town of Rivesaltes on the right-hand side. This is known for its Muscat dessert wines, which come from many of the same properties as the Côtes du Roussillon-Villages. From here go up the valley of the river Agly. At the

village of Cases-de-Pène, turn right, on to the narrow D59. After following the river for a short time and leaving the large Domaine de Jau on the left-hand side, the road winds up into the mountains and reaches the remote village of Tautavel. It was here that the remains of the earliest man in Europe were found.

Behind the co-operative cellar, there is a small Museum of Prehistory.

Beyond Vingrau, the road crosses the river Verdouble and climbs up to arrive in the Aude *département* and the beginning of the Corbières vineyards. These are divided into four regions, all producing different styles of wine.

CANET-EN-ROUSSILLON
Château l'Esparrou 66140 Canet-en-Roussillon Tel:68 73 30 93. (M. or Mme Rendu) Mon-Sat 0900–1300, 1400–2000 Sun 1400–2000. Closed Christmas-New Year. TF.WS. Wine museum. Côtes du Roussillon, Muscat de Rivesaltes.

CASES-DE-PENE
Château de Jau 66600 Cases-de-Pène. Tel:68 64 11 38. (Estelle Daure) Every day 1000–1900. TF.WS.E. 15 Jun-15 Sep Art Exhibition and restaurant by reservation. Côtes du Roussillon, Muscat de Rivesaltes, Banyuls.

TAUTAVEL
Cave de Tautavel, Les Maîtres Vignerons 66720 Tautavel. Mon-Sat 0800–1200, 1400–1800 Sun 1000–1200, 1500–1800. TF.WS. Côtes du Roussillon Villages, Muscat de Rivesaltes.

Vintaging in the Languedoc. The pickers empty their small baskets into the hotte, *the large one on the back of the man on the left. He then empties this into the trailer.*

CAPENDU
Château de Cabriac
Douzens, 11700 Capendu.
Tel:68 77 16 12. (Jean de Cibeins) 0800–1200 by appointment only. TF.WS. Corbières.

LEZIGNAN-CORBIERES
F.L.B. Riga Château du Grand-Caumont, 11200 Lézignan-Corbières. Tel:68 27 10 82. (M. Rigal or M. Blanchard) Every day 0900–1830. TF.WS.E. Beautiful estate. Red Corbières.

MAISONS
Pierre Hodara Domaine Pique-Rouge, 11330 Maisons. Tel:68 70 01 96. By appointment only. TF.WS. The highest vineyard in the Corbières. Red and white Corbières.

PORTEL DES CORBIERES
Domaine de Lastours
11490 Portel des Corbières. Tel:68 48 29 17. (M. Lignères) 0800–1200, 1400–1800, cellar Mon-Fri, château every day. Closed 1st fortnight in Aug. TF.WS. Picnic area.

TUCHAN
Les Caves du Mont Tauch 11350 Tuchan. Tel:68 45 41.08. (Michel Not) Summer, every day, winter, Mon-Fri 0900–1200, 1400–1800. TF.WS.E. Fitou, Corbières, Rivesaltes, Muscat de Rivesaltes.

Corbières
First of all, there are the Coastal Corbières, from the village of Fitou, which gives its name to some of the best wines of the region, to just south of Narbonne. These are soft wines, best drunk young. Then there are the Mountain Corbières planted on stony, chalk soil. These are the fullest-bodied wines, which age well. From around Capendu, in the north-west of the region, come spicier wines, with a fuller bouquet, and finally from around Lézignan, in the valley of the Orbieu, where there are the densest plantings, come wines which have something of all these styles.

If you continue along the road from the Côtes du Roussillon vineyards, you come to the town of Tuchan, overlooked by the magnificent castle of Aguilar, built to guard the frontier between the territories of the Counts of Roussillon and Narbonne.

Here there is a choice. One route takes you to Padern, after which you follow the narrow valley of the Torgan, climb to cross the Col du Prat and join the D613 at Félines, leading to Narbonne. The alternative is to take the D611, through Durban-Corbières, to join the N9 near Portel. Both roads give beautiful views of the rugged local scenery.

Minervois
The vineyards of the Minervois are north of those of the Corbières, on the far bank of the River Aude, between Narbonne and Carcassonne. Here, as in the Corbières, there is some difference between the wines produced in the valley bottom and those from the stony slopes, here called the Haut-Minervois.

The region takes its name from the remote town of Minerve, which stands on a high promontory, where the rivers Cesse and Briant join. Its outstanding feature looks, from a distance, like a factory chimney. In fact it is the small remaining portion of what had been the château wall.

Simon de Montfort

In 1210, the town was one of the last remaining stronghold of the puritan Cathar heretics, who had been attacked by the church, even to the extent of having crusades organized against them. Minerve was besieged by a force led by Simon de Montfort and the Abbot of Cîteaux. After five weeks the town surrendered, when their water supply was cut off.

Simon left it to the Abbot to decide the terms of surrender. The Cathars were to be forgiven if they renounced their heresy and rejoined the church. This they refused to do. 140 of them threw themselves on to the bonfire that was being prepared for them. Three pregnant women were the only ones to be spared.

On another occasion, when asked by one of his soldiers how he could tell the difference between Catholics and Cathars, Simon de Montfort is reputed to have said, 'Kill them all; God will know his own'.

Minerve is on a stony plateau, at the foot of the Montagne Noire, and it is on the slopes up to the plateau that the best wines are made in such villages as Caunes and la Livinière. Most of the wine is red, but more and more drinkable white wines are being made as modern methods of vinification become widely available.

The village of Caunes, once famous for its marble, had an important Benedictine monastery, whose abbey church is now the parish church. At the time of the French Revolution, the bells were melted down and the monastery turned into a prison. Just outside the village is the romanesque chapel of Notre-Dame-du-Cros. Indeed, the region is rich in old churches, that of the village of Rieux dating back to the 12th century.

The Château of Peyrepetuse, one of the last strongholds of the Cathar heretics who defended their faith against the Catholic Church in the 13th century.

In the extreme north-east of the region, on the arid, stony plateau at an altitude of 250 metres, is the village of Saint-Jean-de-Minervois. This has its personal appellation for its dessert wines made from the Muscat grape.

Wine festivals

Spring wine fair, end Apr, Narbonne.
Wine festival Trausse-Minervois, 1st two weeks of July.
Wine festival Minerve, last two weeks of July. Muscat Festival, Aug, Rivesaltes.
Lézignan-Corbières wine festival, 1st fortnight Aug.
Feria, mid Aug, Béziers.

High up in the hills of the Languedoc, the wine of St Chinian is produced, where, as the sign says, it can be tasted in 50 cellars in 20 different villages.

Carcassonne

Just outside the Minervois, to the west, is the city of Carcassonne. The modern town is built in what used to be the suburbs; the old town was built on a limestone hill, overlooking the Aude, and it can still be seen with its complete ring of battlements and towers.

Limoux

Fifteen kilometres (10 miles) south, up the valley of the Aude, is the town of Limoux. This claims to be the earliest centre of sparkling wine production in France. Now, nearly all the wine is made by the co-operative cellar. The Champagne method of sparkling the wine has only been introduced recently, and much is still made by the traditional way of slowing down the first fermentation so that it takes place in the bottle.

Saint-Chinian

In terms of quality, the most important *appellation contrôlée* of the Hérault *département* is Saint-Chinian, named after Aignan, an early bishop of Tours. The vineyards lie on slate soil on both banks of the River Orb,

to the north of Béziers. Only red wine is made from the Grenache, Cinsault and Carignan grapes.

Faugères

The village of Faugères gives its name to a further appellation from the slopes north of Béziers. Here a little white wine is made from the Clairette grape, but most of the production is of a full-bodied red wine. Beyond Faugères there are some beautiful drives in the Monts de l'Espinouse, with views back down to the Mediterranean. There is a small casino at Lamalou les Bains.

Béziers

The city of Béziers is perhaps best known for its rugby team, though it describes itself, rather peculiarly, as 'The Capital of Pure Wine'. Its *Feria*, which takes place in August, features bulls let loose in the streets and a

CAUNES-MINERVOIS
Cave Co-operative de Caunes-Minervois 11160 Caunes. Tel:68 78 00 98. (Philippe Salles) Mon-Fri 0800–1200, 1400–1800. TF.WS.E. Cellars in 16th-century abbey. Red, white and rosé Minervois.
Daniel Domergue Trausse-Minervois, 11160 Caunes-Minervois. Tel:68 78 32 37. (Hélène Domergue) Mon-Fri 0900–1300, 1600–1900. TF.WS.E. Minervois.

LA LIVINIERE
La Cave des Coteaux du Haut Minervois 34210 La Livinière. Tel:68 91 42 67. Mon-Sat 0800–1200, 1400–1800. TF.WS.E. Red, white and rosé Minervois.
Roger Piquet Château de Gourgazaud, 34210 La Livinière. Tel:68 78 10 02. (M. Roux) Mon-Sat 0900–1200, 1400–1700. TF.WS. Minervois. Varietal *vin de pays*.

RIEUX-MINERVOIS
Domaine des Homs 11160 Rieux-Minervois. Tel:68 78 10 51. (Bernard de Crozals) Every day 0800–1200, 1400–1900. TF.WS. Minervois.

MARSEILLAN
Noilly Prat 34340 Marseillan. Tel:67 77 20 15. 1 Apr-10 Oct Mon-Sat 1000–1200, 1420–1830. Rest of year by appointment only. TF.WS.E. Vermouth.

The cellars of the Château de Grezan, near Faugères, some 30 km (20 miles) north of Béziers. There is a restaurant attached to the château.

series of bullfights in the town's bullring.

Along the coast are the modern resort of Valras-Plage, the Bassin de Thau, with its oyster and mussel beds, the old wine port of Sète and, just beyond that, the small town of Frontignan. Dominated as it is by an oil refinery, you would scarcely consider it to be important in the wine world. However, it is the centre of the production of the sweet Muscat de Frontignan and has given its name to a grape variety known world-wide.

Montpellier

There is little doubt that Montpellier has considered itself to be the wine capital of France. In the days when Languedoc was nothing but a sea of vines, it was the centre of that sea. Its university received students of winemaking from all over the world. Now, perhaps, that tide has receded.

The word for the future in Languedoc-Roussillon must be quality. The growers seem to be moving rapidly in the right direction. Tighter controls on production, and the planting of better grape varieties, can only lead to better wine and therefore to more satisfied customers.

MEZE
Abbaye de Valmagne
Villeveyrac, 34140 Mèze.
Tel:67 78 06 09. 15 Jun-15
Sep Wed-Mon 1430–1830.
Rest of year Sun 1400–1800.
Closed during vintage.
TF.WS. 13th-century
abbey with cloisters used as
cellars. Vin de Pays des
Collines de la Mure.

MURVIEL
Guy et Peyre Château
Coujan, 34490 Murviel
Tel:67 37 80 00. (François
Guy) Every day 0900–1200,
1400–1900. St-Chinian.
Coteaux de Murviel.

BANYULS-SUR-MER
S.C.A.E. Parce et Fils
Domaine du Mas Blanc, 9
ave Général de Gaulle,
66650 Banyuls-sur-Mer.
Tel:68 88 32 12. (Jean-
Michel Parce) By
appointment only. TF.WS.

Banyuls, one of the great dessert wines of the French Catalan coast, matures in the summer heat. This treatment give it the oxidized rancio *taste peculiar to wines from this region – on both sides of the frontier.*

The coast road from Spain

There can be few more attractive approaches to France than that on the Mediterranean coast road from Port Bou in Spain. The frontier is on the crest of a hill, overlooking the sea.

The road then winds down to the rather ugly town of Cerbère, dominated by railway sidings. It then climbs again to Cap Rederis; between the road and the sea there is nothing but the railway line, when it has not disappeared into a tunnel, and vines. By some this is called the Côte Vermeille; by others, the Côte Rocheuse, the Rocky Coast. Small

parcels of vines cling to the steep slopes that plunge down to the sea. One wonders how it can be economical to make wine from such vineyards. The fact is that if all the vines were like that, no one could make a living. There are less dramatic places where they are grown.

Apart from Cerbère, the other three towns in the area are Port-Vendres, from where the ferries sail for Algeria, Collioure, an artists' centre, or so the tourists are told, and Banyuls.

Collioure wine

There is a little, full-bodied, spicy red wine made here under the name of Collioure, but the total production has now fallen to less than 50,000 cases a year. Much of this is consumed locally, but if it were imported into Britain, for example, its natural alcoholic strength would pose some problems for the Customs.

V.D.N. wines

The local speciality, however, is the production of what the French call *vins doux naturels*, natural sweet wines, V.D.N. for short. Over 90 per cent of the total production of these wines comes from the Pyrenées-Orientales *depártement*.

They may be called natural wines, but in fact they are not. They are made by adding neutral spirit (brandy is forbidden) to wine must (grape juice) before fermentation is completed, thus killing off the yeasts and capturing the sugar that remains in the wine.

Either red or white wines can be used for this process, and in certain areas the Muscat grape, with its particular flavour. Some of the

The blue Mediterranean reflects the historic port of Collioure.

wines, particularly those made from the Grenache – but never the Muscat – are stored outside in cask, so that the powerful sun can oxidize them. The resultant style is described as *rancio*, and is an acquired taste.

There are four V.D.N. wines made in Roussillon. The finest, and the one with the smallest production, is Banyuls, which comes only from the four towns of the Côte Rocheuse. Here the yields are among the smallest of all the vineyards of France. The finest quality can be called Banyuls Grand Cru and is one of the great fortified wines of the world. It ages well for forty years or more.

The next smallest in terms of production is Maury, from high in the hills of the Côtes du Roussillon, near the beautiful Cathar Château de Quéribus.

Muscat de Rivesaltes is the name of the V.D.N. made just from the Muscat grape, from a hundred villages, all but nine of them in the Pyrenées Orientales, the rest in the Aude. Finally comes Rivesaltes, either red or white, from throughout the region. Anglo-Saxons always seem to have undervalued the V.D.N. wines. Perhaps it is because the French will insist on drinking them before a meal. If only they would try them afterwards!

FOR FURTHER INFORMATION
The Côtes du Roussillon G.I.P.C.R. 19 ave de Grande Bretagne, 66000 Perpignan. Tel:68 51 31 81.
Fitou, Corbières and Minervois Conseil Interprofessionel des Vins de Fitou, Corbières et Minervois, RN 113, 11200 Lézignan-Corbières. Tel:68 27 03 64.
Coteaux du Languedoc Syndicat des Coteaux du Languedoc, Domaine de Maurin, B.P.no 9, 34970 Lattes. Tel:67 27 8411.

Provence _____

One of the most regular problems of the wine merchant is that of holiday wines. At the end of every summer, customers come to him saying, 'I tasted such and such a wine when I was on holiday. It was sensational. Please will you get some of it for me.' Often, these wines are wines from Provence.

There can be few happier memories than that of sitting outside a quayside bar in the south of France, watching the world go by, with a bottle of Côte de Provence rosé in an ice-bucket, and a glass of it in your hand. Sadly, Provence wines are summer wines; sadly, they just do not taste the same in February in Flint, Michigan or Fulham, London.

Nevertheless at the right time and place, on the Riviera in the summer, these wines are enjoyable. Make the most of them while you are there, and visit the vineyards that produce them. Then you will not be disappointed.

Most of the vineyards of Provence lie along the valleys of the rivers Arc and Argens, on the route of the A8 motorway.

Much of the wine is made in co-operative cellars with emotive names like la Prévoyance. Here is made the traditional wine of Provence, a rosé that is high in alcohol and lacking in fruit – whatever defects it may have being masked by the temperature at which it is served.

There is a second band of vineyards along the coast from Marseilles, to Sainte-Maxime and Saint-Tropez. From both these areas comes the ubiquitous Côtes de Provence, too often relying on the novelty of the bottle shape, rather than what is in it, to attract the attention of the consumer.

Nevertheless, there are encouraging signs that growers are beginning to see that the vast captive market of holidaymakers on their doorstep might begin to ask for something rather better. As a result,

less emphasis is being placed on the rosé wines, and those that are made are lighter and crisper, and more on fresh, white wine. The fact that the Côtes de Provence now has *appellation contrôlée* status, with its obligatory tasting, has woken people up.

Red wine, too, is made. The old-fashioned wines are based on the traditional stand-bys of the southern

ST-TROPEZ
Matton-Farnet Château Minuty, Gassin, 83990 St-Tropez. Tel:94 56 12 09. May-Nov every day, Dec-Apr Mon-Fri 0900–1200, 1400–1830. TF.WS.E. Napoléon III chapel. Exhibition of Moustiers faïence.

The picturesque Château Vignelaure in the Coteaux d'Aix-en-Provence (see pages 122-123).

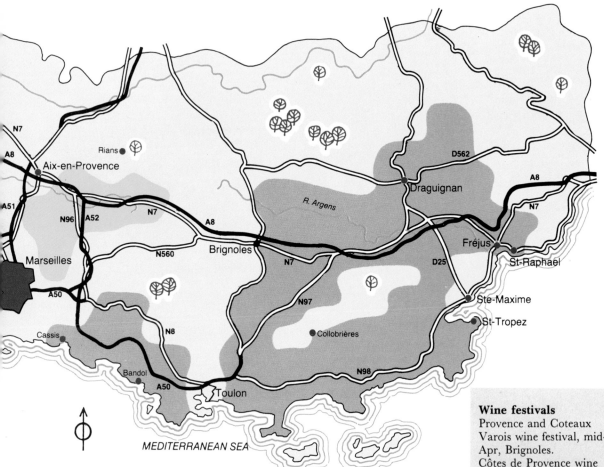

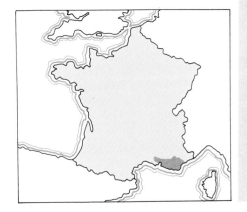

Coteaux d'Aix-en-Provence

Côtes de Provence

French wine grower, the Carignan and the Grenache, and will probably be bottled in the traditional waisted Provence bottle. Growers who have planted better varieties like the Cabernet Sauvignon and the Syrah tend to use Bordeaux bottles. However, this simple test is not an infallible guide to quality! Within the region, there are more individual wines being made. Just raised to a.c. level is the small region of les Coteaux de Baux-en-Provence, to the north-west of Marseilles, close to the town of Arles, renowned for its Roman amphitheatre and its sausages.

Wine festivals
Provence and Coteaux Varois wine festival, mid-Apr, Brignoles.
Côtes de Provence wine festival, mid-Jun, St-Raphael.
Nice wine festival, 1st Sun Aug.
Fréjus wine festival, 2nd weekend Aug.
Ste-Maxime wine festival, 4th weekend Aug.
St-Tropez Harvest Festival, mid-Sep.
Corrida des Vendanges, end Sep, Arles.

To get to Provence
Aix en Provence is 754km (471 miles) from Paris and 97km (60 miles) from Orange on the A6, A7, and A8. It is 145km (90 miles) from Montpellier on the A9, N572, N115, A7 and A8.

Aix-en-Provence is an agreeable centre for visiting the local vineyards. Here, pedestrians stroll beneath the shade of the planes – those most French of urban trees – on the Cours Mirabeau, which leads to the Casino.

Coteaux d'Aix

With a wider reputation, but again recently having gained a.c. status are the wines of the Coteaux d'Aix-en-Provence. Here a number of growers have built up the names of their properties, by planting better grape varieties and by paying close attention to the vinification and ageing of their wines.

Perhaps the best-known among these is Château Vignelaure, near the small town of Rians. This property was bought by Georges Brunet, who had come from Bordeaux, where he had restored to its former glory the long-neglected classified growth, Château La Lagune.

Most of his planting is in the Cabernet Sauvignon of Bordeaux and the Syrah of the Rhône valley, on the theory that the greatest wines came out of Bordeaux when they were liberally dosed with Hermitage, from the Rhône, to give them more body and softness.

To the south of Salon de Provence, close to the Etang de Berre, Denis Langue, at the Château de Calissanne, has come from Burgundy to make excellent wines, his reds with a good base of Cabernet Sauvignon and his whites from a classic blend of Sauvignon and Semillon. Not for him the ageing of red wines in concrete vats: he is experimenting with different types of oak casks.

Château de Fonscolombe

Rather longer in wine-making in the region is the family of the Marquis

RIANS
Château Vignelaure rte de Jouques, 83560 Rians. Tel:94 80 31 93. Mon-Fri 0830–1200, 1400–1800, Sat-Sun 1000–1200, 1400–1800. TF (if you purchase wine). WS.E. Contemporary art exhibition in cellars.

de Saporta, originally from Aragon in Spain. They obtained the property of the Château de Fonscolombe by marriage in 1810. The 170 hectare (over 400 acre) estate lies on chalky-clay soil on the south bank of the river Durance, north of Aix. Here, the top wine is sold as Coteaux d'Aix en Provence, with as much again as Vin de Pays des Bouches du Rhône and ordinary table wine. Less than a sixth of the red vines planted are Cabernet Sauvignon. The rest are the traditional local varieties – Grenache, Carignan and Cinsault.

As an enclave within the area of the Coteaux d'Aix en Provence is the small appellation of Palette. The chalky soil gives fuller bodied wines (red, white and rosé are made) than the rest of the region. The production is small and the one property of note is Château Simone. Little of it seems to go any further than the restaurants of neighbouring Marseilles.

Marseilles
This city was a Greek colony and from the earliest times it was known for its dull, rather heavy, wines, which were useful for blending. Where the Phoenician merchants used to moor their galleys is now the centre of the Vieux Port.

Marseilles has many attractive features, but cannot be described as an attractive city, for the widespread squalor puts off anyone who looks at all closely.

Aix-en-Provence
The same cannot be said about nearby Aix-en-Provence, which was settled by the Romans, largely on account of its warm-water springs. There are many Roman remains in

It seems to be a growing tradition for vineyard owners to commission famous painters to design a different label for them for each vintage. The idea was originated by Baron Philippe de Rothschild at Château Mouton-Rothschild, who, since 1945, has invited such celebrated artists as Chagall, Henry Moore and Salvador Dali to create a new label. One of those to extend this idea has been Georges Brunet at Château Vignelaure, who combines the work of writers and artists on his labels. Here are three examples.

Le vin du Château Vignelaure est présenté par Daniel BOULANGER de l'Académie Goncourt et par le dessinateur Ronald SEARLE.

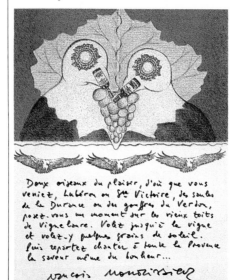

Le Château Vignelaure est présenté par François NOURISSIER de l'Académie Goncourt. Le dessin est de Cécile MUHLSTEIN son épouse.

A TRAVERS LES VERRES DE L'AMITIE, DES REVES NAISSENT DANS CE NOBLE VIN, SAVOUREUX, AUTOMNE, CHATEAU VIGNELAURE.

La récolte Château Vignelaure 1983 est présentée par la poétesse japonaise Michiko Ozima.

the region; to the west, at Saint-Chamas, on the northern shore of the Etang de Berre, is the Pont Flavien.

To the east of the town, in 125 BC, the Roman general Marius gained a major victory over the Cimbri, who are said to have lost 100,000 men on the day. Legend has it that Marius is still one of the most popular names in the area.

Between the vineyards of the valleys of the Arc and the Argens and those of the coast lies the wooded Massif des Maures. From the quiet village of Collobrières, at its centre, there are many beautiful drives.

LANCON-DE-PROVENCE
Château de Calissanne
13680 Lançon-Provence.
Tel:90 42 63 03. Every day
0800–1200, 1400–1800.
TF.WS.

BANDOL
Domaine Tempier
G.A.E.C. Peyraud, Le
Plan de Castellet, 83330 Le
Beausset. Tel:94 98 70 21.
Mon-Fri 0900–1200,
1400–1800. TF.WS.

**LE PUY-STE-
REPARADE**
Château de Fonscolombe
rte de St Canadet, 13610
Le Puy-Ste-Réparade.
Tel:42 61 89 62. Mon-Sat
0800–1200, 1400–1800.
TF.WS.E.

**FOR FURTHER
INFORMATION**
C.I.V.C.P. RN 7, 83460
Les Arcs sur Argens.

The fishing port (above) and the bay (below) of Cassis, not far from Marseilles.

Bandol, Cassis and Bellet

Apart from the wines that have already been mentioned, there are three long-standing a.c. wines, whose reputation – and price – have always stood out from the general mass of the wines of Provence. All three are coastal wines, and all three are largely consumed in the immediate neighbourhood.

The names of the three wines are: Bandol, Cassis and Bellet. Of these, the first is by far the most important, both in terms of production and reputation, but if we continue our geographical progression from west to east, the first one that we come to is Cassis.

Cassis

Almost on the doorstep of Marseilles, Cassis is only 22km (14 miles) away by the D559, which winds across the Col de la Gineste, from where there are beautiful views across to the islands of Calseraigne and Riou.

Cassis itself is a small fishing village tucked away in a small bay. Unfortunately, its proximity to Marseilles means that, particularly at weekends, it is swamped by those coming for the pretty quayside fish restaurants, the casino and the beach. The steep slopes behind, which were once dominated by vines, are being steadily overrun with holiday villas.

For me, the first thing that the word Provence conjures up is herbs, and they seem to appear everywhere in the cookery, sprinkled on meat before it is grilled, in soups, like *soupe au pistou*, or even in the basic provencal sauce. Tomatoes, garlic too, and, of course, olive oil play major rôles in the kitchen.

All of these are ingredients in that Mediterranean speciality, the *bouillabaisse*. To these must be added saffron and a selection of ten or so different fish, plus shellfish. Just as typical is a plate of grilled sardines!

There are certain regional specialities: Aix is known for its sweets, particularly the calissons, Cavaillon for its melons and Arles for its sausages.

Perhaps the best cheeses are those made from goat's milk and then matured, with herbs, in olive oil.

Because of its climate, this is a region of simple cookery. The freshest of raw materials are used. In this part of the world you eat outside: what could be better than a *salad niçoise*, grilled fish, fruit and cheese, washed down by a bottle of chilled wine.

Cassis makes red, white and a little rosé wine, the most distinctive of the three being the white which has a golden straw colour and a vaguely nutty flavour.

Bandol

The area covered by the vineyards of Bandol, which is almost to Toulon what Cassis is to Marseilles, is more than six times as large as that of its neighbour. It also has one considerable advantage: for the most part it is well away from the town itself, and the sea, on rocky, limestone soil.

The basic grape variety is the Mourvèdre, for the red wines, and, by law, these must spend a minimum of eighteen months in wood, generally large oak *foudres*. The result is a full, round, opulent wine that has an immediate appeal when young, like, for example, many Burgundies of the 1985 vintage, but which will, like them, age well.

The red is the best wine, but there is probably more rosé produced, in answer to the regional demand. To my knowledge, this is the only rosé wine which must spend an obligatory time in wood, eight months, and this tends to give it an orange tinge.

The proportion of white wines made is very small, and I must admit that those that I have tasted have had little appeal.

Bellet

I suppose that the most fashionable, and the most crowded, part of the Riviera is that between Cannes and the Italian border.

With the pressures on land, even up into the hills, being so high, it is not surprising that little wine is made – and most is undistinguished, at that.

Nevertheless, there is one minute appellation area, so small that it does not appear on most wine maps. In just two properties in the hills above Nice airport, Bellet is produced in the three colours.

By far the best is the white, but then rarity makes for a high price!

Savoie

DOUVAINE
Stef Mercier Domaine de la Grande Cave de Crépy, Loisin, 74140 Douvaine. Tel:50 94 00 01. (Louis Mercier) Mon-Fri 0800–1730 Sat 0800–1200. Closed Sep. TF (with purchase). WS.E. Historic cellars.

MONTMELIAN
Daniel Fustinoni
Domaine de la Violette, Les Marches, 73800 Montmélian. Tel:79 28 13 30. Mon-Sat 0800–1200, 1400–1800. Closed Oct. TF.WS.

FOR FURTHER INFORMATION
C.I.V.S. 3 rue du Château, 73000 Chambéry. Tel:79 33 44 16.

Wine festival
Savoie Fair, Chambéry, Sep.

The Abbey of Hautecombe, by the side of the Lac du Bourget. The vineyards in the foreground produce wines with the appellation of Marestel.

Of all the vineyard regions of France, that of Savoie is in some ways the most complicated. Indeed, it does not exist as a cohesive group of vines, but rather as a scattering of vineyards in a fish-hook shape, running along the south bank of Lake Geneva, the river Rhône, the Lac du Bourget and the valley of the Isère.

The situation is not made easier, for the wines are named after individual villages, grape varieties, or a combination of the two. While there are some grapes grown, like the Gamay, that are common in the rest of the viticultural world, the majority are purely local varieties or travel under aliases that are difficult to penetrate.

Little of the wine is seen outside the area, for most of it is eagerly consumed in the local ski-resorts of Chamonix, Mégève and Courchevel or in Aix-les-Bains and Chambéry.

Apart from the many variations permitted of Vin de Savoie, there are two villages that have their own *appellation contrôlée*. These are Crépy, on the south shore of Lake Geneva, and Seyssel, on the Rhône to the north of Aix les Bains.

Crépy, which comes in a green *flute* bottle, like that of Alsace, is very low in alcohol and with a refreshing acidity. The grape used is Chasselas, which is generally considered in France to be a table grape. The locals call the wine Crépy *crépitant*; that is, it has a very light sparkle.

The town of Seyssel lies on both banks of the Rhône, with half of it being in the Ain *département* and the rest in Haute-Savoie. Production is divided between still, dry wines and sparkling wine made by the Champagne method. The success of these sparkling wines has overtaken production, and grapes are now brought in from outside the region to make non-a.c. wine.

As for the rest of the wines of Savoie, the rule appears to be that the wine is better if the name of the village appears on the label. Among the better village names are Ayze, Frangy, Chautagne, Marestel, Apremont, Abymes, Chignin, Arbin and Montmélian. These are not to be confused with the grape varieties. Among the lesser-known names here that you might meet are the Altesse (Roussette), Molette, Jacquère and Bergeron in white wines and the

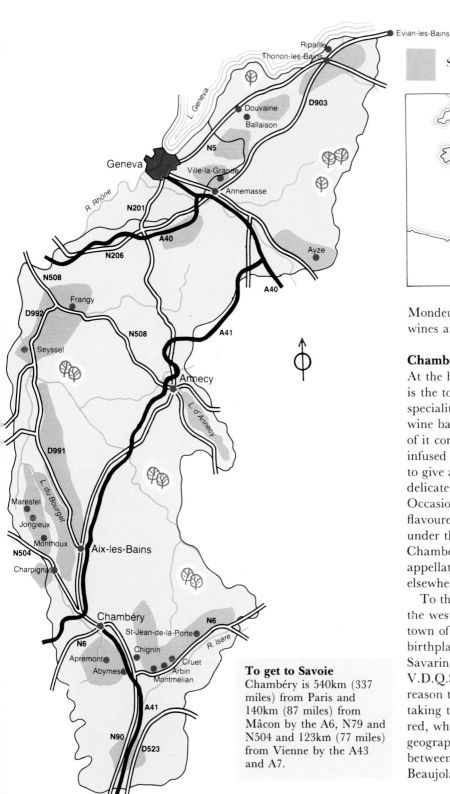

Savoie vineyard area

Mondeuse in red. Nearly all the wines are made to be drunk young.

Chambéry

At the heart of the Savoie vineyards is the town of Chambéry. Here the speciality is vermouth. Originally the wine base was local, but now most of it comes from Italy. Into this is infused a selection of Alpine herbs, to give a vermouth that is much more delicate than those made elsewhere. Occasionally, it can be found flavoured with local strawberries, under the name Chamberyzette. Chambéry vermouth is a protected appellation and cannot be made elsewhere.

To the north-west of Chambéry, on the west bank of the Rhône, is the town of Belley. This was the birthplace of the gastronome Brillat-Savarin. It is also the centre of the V.D.Q.S region of Bugey. For some reason the local growers have resisted taking the a.c. status. The wines, red, white and rosé, reflect their geographical position – somewhere between Savoie, the Jura and the Beaujolais.

To get to Savoie
Chambéry is 540km (337 miles) from Paris and 140km (87 miles) from Mâcon by the A6, N79 and N504 and 123km (77 miles) from Vienne by the A43 and A7.

127

Corsica

Ahundred and sixty years ago, a French writer said of Corsica, 'The vines of this island are remarkable as much for their quality as for the abundance of their fruit. There is very little land where excellent wine can not be obtained, if only it were made with more care.'

The same might be said today, though in between then and now the vineyards on the island were totally destroyed by phylloxera. From that time until the French withdrawal from Algeria, viticulture was in decline.

With the loss of Algeria, two things happened. First of all, there was an immediate need for heavy blending wines to mix with those of the Midi, to fill the traditional French litre bottles of *vin ordinaire*. Secondly, there arrived a number of dispossessed growers from North Africa with money in their pockets. Put the two together and what do you have? Large quantities of very ordinary wine.

The chalk hills of Patrimonio, in northern Corsica. This part of the island produces quality white and rosé wines, as well as full-bodied reds.

This situation could not last, however, for when the Common Market was created, the way was open for large quantities of high-in-alcohol and low-in-price wine from Puglia, and other parts of Italy, to flow into France. As a result, many of the newly-planted Corsican vineyards were grubbed up and replanted with better varieties. Traditionally, for red wines, these have been the local Sciacarello and the Niellucio. (The latter is a close relative of the Sangiovese of Tuscany.) Also from the mainland have come such southern grape varieties as the Grenache, the Syrah and the Mourvèdre. White wines are made mainly from the Vermentino and the Ugni Blanc.

Anyone looking at a map of the island will see that the dominant feature is the mountains, which come down steeply to the sea, except from one part of the eastern side, where there is a plain up to 16km (10 miles) wide. It was on this plain that many of the larger vineyard properties were created. The best wines, however, come from vineyards planted on the slopes.

Much of the wine is sold as *vin de pays*, vin de pays de l'Ile de Beauté, that is. The best wines, however, are entitled to the *appellation contrôlée* Vin de Corse and there are a number of regional names that can be added to this.

These are as follows, working in a clockwise direction from the northern tip of the island:

Coteaux de Cap Corse (not to be confused with the local aperitif of the same name). Here the most striking wine is a *vin doux naturel* made from Muscat grapes, often laid out on mats to gain extra sweetness.

Patrimonio The oldest a.c. on the island. Here the chalky soil gives deep purple wines with a great deal of complexity, perhaps the best on the island.

Porto-Vecchio from the south-east of the island. Generally the best white wines.

Figari The southern tip of Corsica is very rugged. Excellent red wines with much character are made here.

Sartène Elegant red, white and rose wines, produced on granitic soil.

Coteaux d'Ajaccio Similar wines to those of the southern Côtes du Rhône.

Calvi Simple wines that should be drunk young. The whites, particularly, tend to lack acidity. Some medium-sweet wines are also made in the region.

Over the past few years, the wines of Corsica have moved dramatically in the right direction. Because of transport problems, few of them will leave the island. They are, however, worth seeking out.

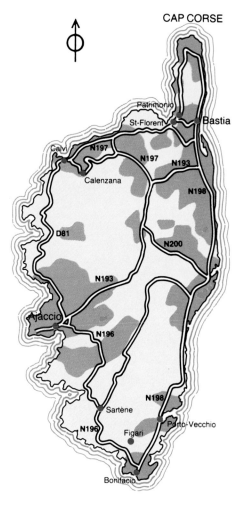

Corsica vineyard area

AJACCIO
Guy de Poix Domaine Peraldi, chemin du Stiletto, 20167 Mezzavia, Ajaccio. Tel:95 22 37 30. Mon-Sat 0800–1200, 1400–1800. TF.WS.E. All wines have won medals. Large fresco. Vin de Corse Ajaccio.

CALENZANA
Tony Orsini Domaine de Rochebelle, 20214 Calenzana. Tel:95 62 81 01. Every day 0800–2000. TF.WS.E. Vin de Corse Calvi, sparkling wine, aperitifs, liqueurs, jams.

PORTO-VECCHIO
Christian Imbert Domaine de Torraccia, Lecci, 20137 Porto-Vecchio. Tel:95 71 43 50. Mon-Sat 0800–1200, 1400–1800. TF.WS.E. Beautiful site. Vin de Corse Porto-Vecchio.

FOR FURTHER INFORMATION Groupement Interprofessionel des Vins de l'Ile de Corse, 6 rue Gabriel Péri, 20000 Bastia. Tel:96 31 37 36.

Eating in France

One of the greatest pleasures of travelling in France is that of tasting the broad range of foods that is available. The French are interested in what they eat and drink, and this shows at all levels. One other important point is that children are welcome in all but the smartest restaurants and it is quite acceptable to ask for an extra plate for a meal to be shared – though sometimes there is a charge for this.

Even when travelling on the motorways, it is possible to eat well, and also to drink well – provided you are not driving – for wine and beer can be served if you take a meal. There are a number of chains of roadside restaurants and Courte-Paille and Les 4 Pentes can be recommended for simple grills.

Shopping for food

If you want to picnic, you can probably buy all that you want in a supermarket, but if you want to buy everything at the specialist shops, these are the ones to look out for:
Boulangerie: the baker's. The traditional French loaf is a *baguette*, a *ficelle* is a long thin one and a *miche* is a round one, often made of less refined flour. A roll is a *petit pain*.
Charcuterie: the pork-butcher's. Here you can buy a broad range of pâtés and sausages. Pâtés can be bought by the slice. Often there is also a range of prepared dishes like pizzas and *coq au vin*. These can be useful if you are doing your own cooking. If you want takeaway food, the phrase to look out for is *plats à emporter*.

Fruit, vegetables, cheese, wine and water can be bought at the ubiquitous general stores. If you buy wine, or water, in litre glass bottles, it will work out cheaper – if you return the bottles.

Bars and restaurants

As in other countries, there is a broad range of places at which you can eat. The word for snack is *casse-croute*, and these are available in most bars. Most frequently offered are sandwiches, comprising a large slice of French bread with cheese, pâté or ham. Unless you ask for it there will not be any butter. Also widely available is the *croque-monsieur*, a welsh rarebit, with a slice of ham.

Moving up a stage, there is the *brasserie*, which is generally attached to a bar. Here you can eat a complete meal or just one dish. Normally, there is just one set meal and a large choice *à la carte*. This can be very convenient if there are widely varying appetites in the party, or for feeding children, for food is served all through the day. An alternative is the *self*, or self-service restaurant, but generally these are only found in the larger towns.

Regional specialities

In certain regions there are regional speciality snacks, which can make for cheap eating. For example, in Brittany go to a *crêperie*, where you can have savoury and sweet pancakes, with a broad range of fillings, and a bottle of cider as an economical meal. Similarly, in Alsace, seek out the *tarte flambée*, which is the local equivalent of the pizza.

Restaurants come in a broad variety of styles and prices. First of all, I would suggest that ethnic restaurants, with the possible exception of Italian ones, should be avoided. However much you enjoy Chinese food, for example, I would suggest that you leave it alone in France.

Relais Routiers

For economical eating, but good food, it is useful to look out for the sign of the Relais Routiers. Though aimed specifically at truck-drivers, these restaurants offer very good food at reasonable prices. Whilst the ambiance may not be quite what you are looking for, the food will make up for it. Indeed, it is not a bad idea to look out for those places with a lot of lorries outside; the French truck driver places a much higher premium on what he eats than his English equivalent.

The menu

Somewhat confusingly, the French word for menu is *carte*. *Le menu* means a set meal (as opposed to the *à la carte* selection). Most restaurants in France will display their menus outside, so it is often possible to do some window shopping, before making a choice. Again there will normally be a selection of menus at a variety of prices. Often there will be a 'tourist' menu (*menu touristique)* at a basic price which will include a drink; wine, beer or mineral water. Sometimes this is hidden away at the back, because, whilst the restaurateur is obliged, by law, to offer it, he is less interested in selling it as he makes a smaller profit. The motto should be, 'seek, and you shall find'.

There may well be a variety of four or five differently-priced menus on offer, each with a broad variety of dishes. Frequently, nowadays, one comes across a *menu dégustation*, which will include several dishes, but only small quantities of each. This gives you an opportunity of tasting a wide range of the specialities of the restaurant.

At the other extreme is the *ménu gastronomique*. This will be more expensive, and as the higher price reflects quantity as well as quality, it should not be attempted by the faint-hearted.

Eating à la carte

In addition to the variety of set menus, there will be an *à la carte* selection. This can be useful if you do not want to eat too many courses, but it is generally a more expensive way of eating and, if you do your sums carefully, you may find that you get an extra course free of charge if you take one of the menus. If you eat *à la carte* you may also have to pay a cover charge which would be included in the menu.

By law, restaurant prices now must include any service charge, though it is normal to round up what you pay at the end of the meal.

Finally, here are a few random thoughts. In certain of the cheaper restaurants you might be expected to keep your knife and fork between courses. You will almost certainly be offered mineral water, *plate* for still or *gazeuse* for fizzy. If you are happy with tap water – and it is safe throughout France – ask for *une carafe d'eau*. Cheese is served before the dessert, not after it and, finally, whilst the word *crème* does mean cream, it is not often served. *Crème fraiche* is sour cream, rather than fresh and *crème anglaise* is custard!

Bon appetit.

French Cheeses

Cheese and wine have long been noted as ideal partners, and it is fitting that France should be almost as well known for the variety of cheeses that it produces as for its variety of wine.

It was General de Gaulle who said, 'It is only under the threat of danger that the French will be united. You can't easily bring together a country that has two hundred and sixty-five individual cheeses.' I am not sure where he found that figure, but I am certain that it would now be much larger, with the introduction of many commercial brands of cheese in addition to the traditional ones.

The range of styles of cheese available is broad, and while you might expect to find certain cheeses – Camembert for example – on almost every cheese-board, there are others that have only a regional importance. Interesting, too, is the fact that certain cheeses have their own *appellations controlées*, with strict regulations as to where and how they might be produced. Others, and again Camembert is an example, can be produced anywhere, though they will maintain their characteristics wherever their source.

Here is a short list of some of the better-known cheeses of France, and of some of my special favourites. It is always worthwhile asking the waiter, or the shop assistant, about the different cheeses available. In a restaurant, do not hesitate to ask for a selection of cheeses from the board. This will give you an opportunity of making a comparative tasting. One word to look out for, with regard to cheese, is *fermier*. This means that it is farm – as opposed to factory – produced and should have more flavour.

Banon (Provence. Cow, sheep or goat.) A small round cheese, wrapped in chestnut leaves. Mild tasting.

Bleu de Gex (Jura. Cow.) A round disc with a hard rind. The cheese is solid with a rich blue vein running through it. It can be fairly strong.

Bresse Bleu (Bresse, across the Saône from the Beaujolais. Cow.) A blue cheese in the shape of a small drum. It comes in a variety of sizes and is similar to a Gorgonzola.

Brie (Ile de France. Cow.) One of the classic cheeses of France. It comes in the form of a large flat disc. Similar in texture to a Camembert. There are a number of regional varieties. Brie de Meaux is one of the best.

Brillat-Savarin (Normandy. Cow.) A very rich, mild, cheese, high in fat content, with a buttery texture.

Camembert (Normandy. Cow.) Though coming originally from Normandy, this is now made almost everywhere in France, and, indeed, throughout the world. It is a round cheese with a white downy rind and a fairly mild taste.

Cancoillotte (Franche-Comté. Cow.) This is a local speciality used for spreading. It has a full flavour.

Cantal (Auvergne. Cow.) Similar in shape and flavour to a large farmhouse Cheddar.

Carré de l'Est (Lorraine. Cow.) A smallish, square cheese with a white rind. Rather neutral flavour.

Chabichou (Poitou. Goat.) The shape of a small cone with the point cut off. It has a white downy rind and a pronounced goaty flavour.

Chaource (Champagne. Cow.) Rather like a much thicker Camembert. It has a pleasant chalky flavour.

Chavignol (Sancerre. Goat.) In the form of a small disc, it has a pleasantly soft, nutty, taste.

Comté (Franche-Comté. Cow.) Often known locally as Gruyère or Emmental, they are just what it is like – a large flavoursome Swiss cheese with holes.

Epoisses (Burgundy, Cow.) A highly-flavoured cheese with an orange rind, which is often washed with the local brandy to give it its individuality.

Gaperon (Auvergne. Cow.) In the shape, and approximate size, of half a tennis-ball, this cheese tastes distinctly of the garlic with which it is flavoured.

Livarot (Normandy. Cow.) Approximately the size and shape of a Camembert. It is distinguished by its brown rind and the 'stripes' of sedge-grass with which it is bound. It has a strong smell and a full, spicy taste.

Maroilles (Flanders. Cow.) A spherical, Dutch-style cheese.

Munster (Alsace, Cow.) One of the most pungent-smelling cheeses of France. Whilst it has a full flavour, its bite is by no means as bad as its bark. In Alsace it is often served with caraway seeds.

Pont l'Evêque (Normandy. Cow.) A small square cheese with a golden skin, a rich yellowish texture and full, nutty taste.

Reblochon (Savoie. Cow.) This is a smallish circular cheese, with a deep yellow rind and a mild, creamy taste.

Roquefort (Plateau of Larzac. Sheep.) The classic blue cheese of France, which is matured for at least three months in the naturally damp caves of Cambalou. It has a very full flavour.

Saint-Paulin (Western France.

Cow.) This is a generic cheese made widely in France, based on the monk's cheese of Port-Salut. It has an orange rind and a soft, mild taste.

Bread, cheese, wine and fruit; the ideal end to a meal – or the basic ingredients of a picnic.

133

If not Wine, What?

Whilst this book is primarily about vineyards, and wine drinking, there are regions of France where wine is of secondary importance, and, no matter where you go, there is almost certain to be a local speciality other than the wine.

Beer
As you drive from the Channel ports of north-east France, for example, you are in beer country. The beers of which they are proudest are the *bières de garde*, which are bottled with Champagne corks and are high in alcohol for long keeping.

In a French bar, there are generally two kinds of bottled beer, *une blonde*, which is a lager, and *une brune*, which is a darker, more fully-flavoured, beer. There is often draught lager and the normal order is *un demi à pression*, which will give you a 25cl. glass. A shandy is *une panachée*.

The other alcoholic speciality of the region is gin distilled from beet. This comes in two forms, young and aged. I must admit to having no experience of it, but I am told that if you want to try the aged variety, a Vieux Loos is as acceptable as anything!

Alsace is the other big region for beer drinking – the skyline of the northern suburbs of Strasbourg is dominated by brewery buildings.

Cider
Normandy and Brittany make up the apple country and cider is widely drunk. Generally speaking, this is drier, and stronger, than the English equivalent (and, for American readers, I should point out that in Europe cider is always what you call 'hard' cider). Better qualities are sold in a corked bottle and are known as *cidre bouché*.

Mineral water
One important drink in France, which must not be forgotten, is mineral water. Whilst tap water is always drinkable, and can be ordered in a restaurant by asking for *une carafe d'eau*, bottled water is widely drunk.

In the supermarkets, there is a broad range available in both glass and plastic bottles. A deposit will be paid on the glass, but this is refundable.

In restaurants, the choice is generally restricted to a few well-known, national brands. Local waters are not often offered, with the possible exception of in Alsace, where Carola, from Ribeauvillé, either still or sparkling, is widely available.

Generally, the choice in waters is between still and sparkling. For those who want a clean neutral tasting still water, I would suggest Evian. Alternatives are Contrexéville (commonly called Contrex), Vittel Grande Source and Volvic.

Of the sparkling water, Perrier is perhaps the most common, though, for those who like rather less aggression in their fizz, I would suggest the more gentle Badoit, from Saint Galmier in the Loire Valley.

Brandy
Returning to the world of alcohol, every wine-producing region has its local brandies. In Burgundy, for example, there are the Marc de Bourgogne and the Fine Bourgogne. The first is distilled from the *marc*, or residue of skins and pips after pressing, and the latter from the lees, or deposit in the wine. Marc is much

more highly flavoured than Fine and can be an acquired taste. Other local marcs of note are the Marc de Champagne and Marc de Provence.

Wherever fruit is grown, alcoholic drinks are produced. For the most part these are of two kinds. If the fruit itself is allowed to ferment and is then distilled, the result is an *alcool blanc*, or white spirit. These are produced widely in France, but the finest probably come from the Giessen valley in Alsace. Here, in just a few kilometres, eleven distilleries produce a broad range from raw materials as varied as cherries (kirsch), raspberries (framboise), plums (quetsch and mirabelle) and holly berries (houx). Other centres of production of fine *alcools blancs* include Fougerolles, in the Vosges, the Rhône valley and St-Jean-Pied-de-Port in the foothills of the Pyrenees.

Liqueurs

Fruit and herbs can also be macerated in alcohol to produce liqueurs – and these are produced all over France. There are certain regional specialities such as the Crème de Cassis (blackcurrant) and Crème de Prunelle (sloe) of Burgundy and the Génépi (herbs) of the Alps, but there are many companies throughout France, each producing its own range of products. In certain cases, the outstanding brand has managed to create an international reputation for itself. Many of these liqueur distilleries can be visited.

Here are some of the more famous names, available throughout France:

Bénédictine (Produced at Fécamp, in Normandy). A sweet liqueur flavoured basically with herbs

growing on the local cliffs. A drier version, originally for the American market, is B & B, which has brandy added to it.

Chartreuse (Voiron in the Alps). This is a sophisticated form of *génépi* distilled by the Carthusian monks. It comes in two forms, yellow, which is high strength, and green, which is very high strength. There is also a small amount of old-aged Chartreuse on the market.

Clacquesin (Paris). A liqueur flavoured with pine-needles.

Cointreau (Angers). This is the most successful of the triple-sec curaçaos. The basic flavour comes from the distilled essence of bitter orange peel.

Grand Marnier (Paris). Another form of curaçao, but using brandy as the base spirit.

Izarra (Bayonne). This is the Basque word for star and has a base of Armagnac, flavoured with herbs and honey from the Pyrenees. It comes in both yellow and green varieties.

Marie Brizard (Bordeaux). Whilst this company makes a range of liqueurs and perhaps the top-selling French gin, it is best-known for its anisette, or sweet aniseed flavoured liqueur.

Verveine de Velay (Le Puy). Made by the Pagès company, which is also known for its herbal teas, this is based on verbena – and an assortment of other herbs.

A final family in the French world of drinks is that of the pastis and anis apéritifs, which turn cloudy when water is added to them.

Vieille Curé (Bordeaux.) Of monastic origins, a herbal liqueur, with Cognac and Armagnac brandies as its base.

Buying Wine in France

One of the pleasures of visiting vineyards is that of buying wine, whether it be for the picnic lunch that day or to fill the boot of your car for further enjoyment when you return home. Here are a few simple hints.

If you are just buying a single bottle for a picnic, you are unlikely to go too far wrong. However, it is as well to remember that simple food is best accompanied by simple wine. For example, if you are in Burgundy, I would not suggest that you bought anything much more complicated than a Beaujolais, a Mâcon Blanc or perhaps a Bourgogne Aligoté to accompany your *déjeuner sur l'herbe*. The chances of your being able to present, say, a Beaune *premier cru* at its best are small. While it might taste excellent, it deserves better treatment.

Supermarkets

Do not despise the French supermarkets as a source of wine. Over the past few years, they have come to realise that they are capable of selling even the finest wines – and they generally do so more cheaply than even a grower would.

It is always worthwhile looking along the supermarket shelves, for there are often excellent bargains to be found in top quality wines from reputable sources.

How about buying wines to bring home? Not very long ago, there were a number of wines that were described as 'not being able to travel'. As a class, they no longer exist (if they ever did) but – you should always ask yourself whether it is worth letting the wine travel in the first place!

Before you invest in a wine, try to imagine what it will taste like when you get it home. Far too often, people are disappointed when they later drink what they thought was a sensational wine in a little bar on the water front of a small Mediterranean port, or in some small grower's cellar in the Loire Valley.

Wine on holiday

Two things go to make up the pleasure of drinking a wine. One is the intrinsic quality of the wine itself. The other is the atmosphere in which it is drunk. Far too often, as far as 'holiday' wines are concerned, the second consideration plays too large a part when decisions to purchase are made.

It is no great coincidence that, for example, everyone seems to enjoy Rosé de Provence in the South of France, but that sales of it are minimal in Britain and the United States. The wines are good, but they exist in a 'frame' that enhances them, perhaps a little too much. Take them out of that frame and they appear much less attractive.

Another point to consider in a similar light is the quantity of wine that you are going to purchase. I would suggest that when you have decided on the total quantity of wine you wish to take home, you split it between more than one wine. The reason is simple: there is much less chance of the wines being a total disappointment.

Bulk buying

I would also be wary of buying wine in bulk, either in the small plastic barrel, which is becoming more and more widespread in France, or else in a 'cubitainer', which is something like a large 'bag-in-box' and which normally holds about 18 litres.

In France, these wines are bought for home bottling or large parties, rather than as a regular source of wine on draught. The problem is that they only give limited protection to the wine. As soon as any has been drawn out of the container, there is a real danger that what remains will 'go off' after a short time.

Personally, I always find it safer to buy wine in a proper bottle with a proper cork.

Buying direct

If you are buying wine direct from a grower or merchant, as opposed to a retail shop, there are two ways that you can go about it. These are known as *en acquit* and *en c.r.d.*

Buying wine *en c.r.d.*

As it is the more general way of buying wine, let us deal with the second method first.

This basically means that you buy the wine having paid all the taxes in France. These include the duty on the wine, which amounts to a few centimes per bottle, and the Value Added Tax (or T.V.A., as it is known) which, at the time of writing, amounts to 18.6 per cent. The fact that the wine has had the duty paid on it is shown by the capsule, which will have a small official 'stamp' on the top.

When you buy wine in this way, you are entitled to the maximum amount of duty-free allowance when you return to Britain. It is interesting to note that this figure, for wine at least, seems to be increasing steadily, and that the customs officer will frequently allow you twice as much free of duty if you have no spirits. Don't, however, count on his invariable generosity.

Buying wine *en acquit*

Often growers and merchants are not happy about selling wine *en acquit* to someone they do not know, as they can have a considerable amount of trouble with the authorities if the buyer does not do all that is necessary. If you buy your wine in this way, you pay neither the French duties, nor the T.V.A. However you have to state where and when you are leaving the country.

When you leave France, you must go to the customs and give them one of the accompanying documents and do the same thing when you arrive in Britain, where you will have to pay the British V.A.T and duty. If you do not complete all the necessary formalities, you too can find authority descending upon you when you least expect it!

Simply put, it is only worthwhile buying *en acquit* if you are buying a number of cases of wine.

Vintages

In most cellars, in most regions of France, you will generally be offered wines of the latest vintage. The further south you go, the less difference there is likely to be between the vintages. However, in areas such as Burgundy, there might be considerable variations in quality from year to year.

Recent improvements in techniques in both the vineyards and the wine-cellars have meant that there is little chance of a truly disastrous vintage, as far as quality is concerned. In the best years, bad wines are made – and vice-versa. I would recommend that you taste before you buy and that you pay more attention to what the grower says than to a vintage chart.

The Top 21 Grape Varieties

Aligoté (white). A secondary grape in Burgundy, where it gives the early-drinking Bourgogne Aligoté.

Cabernet Franc (black). A secondary grape in Bordeaux; more important in the Loire valley, where it produces most of the better red wines like Chinon and Saumur-Champigny.

Cabernet Sauvignon (black). One of the world's great grape varieties. The basis of the great wines of the Médoc, it gives wines full of fruit and tannin, which age well.

Carignan (black). At present, the most widely planted wine grape variety in France, mainly in the Midi. Generally speaking the wine it gives is undistinguished.

Chardonnay (white). Now a world-wide favourite. The quality white grape in Burgundy and Champagne, where it gives full-bodied wines which are capable of ageing.

Chasselas (white). Largely a table grape. Grown in France for winemaking in Pouilly-sur-Loire and, in decreasing quantities, in Alsace.

Chenin Blanc (white). Also known as the Pineau de la Loire. Used for making all the great sweet wines of the Loire valley, as well as most of the dry ones.

Gamay (black). The grape of the Beaujolais, where it gives a refreshing wine full of fruit.

Gewürztraminer (white). Grown in Alsace, where it gives an individual, spicy wine, often high in alcohol.

Grenache (black or white). Originally a Spanish variety, now widely planted throughout all the vineyard regions of the French Mediterranean.

Merlot (black). The second grape of Bordeaux and the basis of the great wines of Saint-Emilion and Pomerol.

Muscadet (white). Also known as the Melon de Bourgogne. The grape that produces the Muscadet wines of Brittany. Generally speaking, the wines are refreshing, slightly acid, and low in alcohol.

Muscat (white). A highly perfumed grape that is used to make many of the sweet dessert wines of the south of France. In Alsace it gives a full-flavoured dry wine.

Pinot Blanc (white). A high-yielding vine making a simple refreshing wine lacking a great deal of character. In Alsace, it is sometimes called the Clevner.

Pinot Gris (white). Grown in a broad range of French vineyards, under a variety of names. In Alsace it is the Tokay; in Champagne, the Fromentot; in Burgundy, the Pinot Beurot and in the Loire valley, the Malvoisie. The wines are generally soft and appealing, low in acidity and often high in alcohol.

Pinot Noir (black). Makes the great red wines of Burgundy and is widely grown in Champagne.

Riesling (white). In France, is grown just in Alsace, where it gives magnificent, full, steely, dry wines.

Sauvignon Blanc (white). Now widely planted in Bordeaux where it is the basis of the best dry white wines. Its finest wines are probably those of Sancerre and Pouilly-Fumé.

Semillon (white). Used to produce the sweet wines of south-west France, such as Sauternes and Monbazillac.

Sylvaner (white). The most widely planted grape in Alsace. It gives a simple, rather earthy wine.

Syrah (black). The quality wine of the Rhône valley. Now also being planted widely to improve many of the wines of the Midi.

Glossary of Wine Terms

Appellation contrôlée (a.c.) the highest regional classification for French wines.

Barrique a barrel.

Brut very dry, particularly of sparkling wines.

Brut nature totally dry. No residual sugar.

Cave a cellar.

Caveau a tasting-cellar.

Chai a wine-warehouse above ground, particularly in Bordeaux.

Clairet a deep rosé or light red wine.

Clos a vineyard enclosed by a wall.

Cru a growth, often used in terms of classification; thus, in Burgundy, *un grand cru* or *un premier cru*.

Cuve a vat.

Cuvée a selected vat, eg *cuvée exceptionelle*.

Demi-sec medium-sweet; generally more sweet than medium.

Feuillette a half-size cask of about 112 litres, particularly in Chablis and Burgundy.

Flûte a tall, slim bottle used in Alsace; a narrow Champagne glass.

Foudre a large oak cask used in Alsace and the South of France for ageing wine.

Frais cool.

Frappé chilled (of Champagne).

Glacé iced (of Champagne).

Millésime vintage.

Mise en bouteille au Château bottled at the Château (Bordeaux).

Mise en bouteille au Domaine bottled at the Domain (Burgundy).

Moelleux sweet.

Mousseux sparkling.

Pétillant lightly sparkling.

Phylloxera an aphid that destroyed most European vineyards during the last century. Almost all vines are now grafted on to American rootstock, which are resistant to this insect.

Pièce a cask, particularly in Burgundy: 225 litres in the Côte d'Or; rather less in the Beaujolais.

Pourriture Noble (Botrytis cinerea) a type of fungus that attacks ripe grapes in certain vineyard areas. It increases the sugar content of the grapes, which are used for making the finest sweet wines, eg Sauternes.

Rancio a wine that is aged in the sun and becomes oxidized; a speciality of the Catalan vineyards, in both France and Spain.

Sec dry.

Sélection de grains nobles the highest quality level in Alsace wines theoretically made from hyper-ripe, individually picked grapes.

Sur lie literally 'on the lees'. A way of bottling some wines from the Muscadet and elsewhere, where the wines are young and unfiltered so as to give them extra fruit and freshness. Often there is a small amount of residual gas in the wine.

Tonneau a large cask. In Bordeaux, equal to four *pièces*, ie 900 litres.

V.D.Q.S. (vin délimité de qualité supérieure) The highest status for French wines after *appellation contrôlée (a.c.)*.

Vendange Tardive literally 'late harvest': a term denoting quality, used for Alsace wines.

Vin de paille 'straw wine'. A very sweet wine where the grapes, after picking, are left on straw to ripen further. Now made in minute quantities in the Jura.

Vin de pays a classification below V.D.Q.S., where the wine comes from a specific region.

Vin de table table wine. The lowest classification of French wine.

Vin doux naturel (V.D.N.) a sweet dessert wine, often made in the South of France from the Muscat grape.

Further Information

METRIC EQUIVALENTS		
Kilometres		**Miles**
1.61	1	0.62
3.22	2	1.24
4.83	3	1.86
6.44	4	2.49
8.05	5	3.11
9.66	6	3.73
11.27	7	4.35
12.88	8	5.59
14.48	9	5.59
64.37	10	6.21
80.47	50	31.07
96.56	60	37.28
112.65	70	43.50
128.75	80	49.71
144.84	90	55.92
160.93	100	62.14

Hectares		**Acres**
0.41	1	2.47
0.81	2	4.94
1.21	3	7.41
1.62	4	9.88
2.02	5	12.36
2.43	6	14.83
2.83	7	17.30
3.24	8	19.77
3.64	9	22.24
4.05	10	24.71
8.09	20	49.42
12.14	30	74.13
16.19	40	98.84
20.23	50	123.56
24.28	60	148.26
28.33	70	172.97
32.37	80	197.68
36.42	90	222.40
40.47	100	247.11

Tourist Offices

Look for the sign *Syndicat d'Initiative*. These offices can often help with vineyard visits and hotel accommodation. They are pleased to give advice on local events, amenities and excursions and can also answer specific local queries such as bus timetables and local religious services (all denominations). Sometimes, too, they have currency exchange facilities out of banking hours. In popular resorts, *Syndicats d'Initiative* are sometimes open late and on Sunday mornings. Here is a list of some of the main offices:

Aix-en-Provence pl Général de Gaulle. Tel:42 24 20 41.
Angers gare St-Laud. Tel:41 87 72 50.
Auxerre 2 quai Republique. Tel:86 52 06 19.
Avignon 41 cours Jean-Jaurès. Tel:90 82 65 11.
Beaune face Hôtel-Dieu. Tel:80 22 24 51.
Bordeaux 12 cours XXX juillet. Tel:56 44 28 41.
Carcassone bd Camille-Pelletelan. Tel:68 25 68 81.
Chambéry pl Mong. Tel:79 33 42 47.
Cognac pl François 1er. Tel:45 82 10 71.
Colmar 4 rue Unterlinden. Tel:89 41 02 29.
Dijon pl Darcy. Tel:80 43 42 12.
Mâcon ave de Lattre de Tassigny. Tel:85 38 06 00.
Montpellier, pl Comédie. Tel:67 72 54 82.
Reims 3 bd Paix. Tel:26 47 25 69.
Saint-Emilion pl des Creneaux. Tel:56 24 72 03.
Strasbourg 10 pl Gutenberg. Tel:88 32 57 07.
Tours pl Gare. Tel:47 05 58 08.

Accueil de France

A further source of information within the country is the *Accueil de France* ('French Welcome Office'). These offices will also book hotel reservations within their area for the same night or up to seven days in advance *for personal callers only*. There are not so many of these offices and they are located mainly at important stations and airports.

The hours of opening vary considerably depending upon the district and the time of year. Generally the offices are open between 0900–1200 and 1400 to 1800 from Monday to Saturday..

Shopping hours

Department stores are usually open from Monday to Saturday 0900–1830/1900, closing for lunch only in the provinces.

Food shops normally open at 0700 and may also open on Sunday mornings.

Public Holidays in France

January 1st (New Year's Day)
Easter Monday
1 May (Labour Day)
Ascension Day
Monday after Pentecost
14 July (Bastille Day)
15 August (Assumption)
1 November (All Saints Day)
11 November (Armistice Day)
25 December (Christmas Day)

If a Public Holiday falls on a Tuesday or a Thursday, there is a growing tendency to *faire le pont*, (bridge the gap) and take the intervening day off too. Much of France, particularly Paris, closes down for the whole of August.

Sample letter to a grower

[Sender's name, address and telephone number]

[Date]

Madame/Monsieur*, [either or both]

Ayant relevé vos coordonnées dans le 'Travellers Wine Guide - France', j'aimerais visiter vos caves et installations le [date] aux environs de [time].

Je serai probablement accompagné de [number] personnes/d'une autre personne*.
[*The above paragraph is optional.*]

Si cela ne vous convient pas, je vous serais reconnaissant de bien vouloir me le faire savoir, soit par courrier à l'adresse ci-dessus, soit en m'appelant au [telephone number].

Je vous prie d'agréer, madame/monsieur*, l'expression de mes meilleurs sentiments.

[Signature]

Dear Madame/Sir*,

Having read the particulars of your establishment in the *Travellers Wine Guide – France*, I should like to visit your cellars on [date] at about [time].

I shall probably be accompanied by [number] other people/one other person*

If this arrangement is not convenient to you, I should be most grateful if you could contact me by letter or telephone.

Yours sincerely,

[Signature]

* *delete where not applicable.*

Using a French telephone

Outside Paris, all French telephone numbers have eight digits, of which the first two represent the *département* (administrative district). Telephones in Paris and nearby have nine digits of which the first is always 1.

If you are making a call within the *département*, just dial the number. If you are telephoning anywhere else in France, dial 16, wait for another dialling tone and then dial the number. To telephone abroad, similarly dial 19 and wait for the second dialling tone. For calls from abroad, the international code for France is 33.

In most French telephone boxes, there are detailed instructions in English. A variety of coins can be used and the machine takes these beginning with those of the lowest value and returning any unspent coins at the end of the call.

Further Reading

Of the vast number of books on French wine, I can recommend Alexis Lichine's *Guide to the Wines and Vineyards of France* (Papermac) as a good general guide.

At a fairly simple yet instructive level, I would suggest the Century Companion range of books on Burgundy, Champagne and Cognac. More detailed are the Mitchell Beazley Pocket Guides series, which includes titles on Burgundy and Bordeaux.

Mitchell Beazley are also the publishers of Hugh Johnson's monumental *World Atlas of Wine*.

Two publications that the motorist will find particularly useful are the *Michelin Road Atlas – France* (Paul Hamlyn) and the *AA Travellers' Guide to Europe.*

METRIC EQUIVALENTS		
Litres		Imperial Gallons
4.55	1	0.22
9.09	2	0.44
13.64	3	0.66
18.18	4	0.88
22.73	5	1.10
27.28	6	1.32
31.82	7	1.54
36.37	8	1.76
40.91	9	1.98
45.46	10	2.20
90.92	20	4.40
136.38	30	6.60
181.84	40	8.80
227.30	50	11.00
272.76	60	13.20
318.22	70	15.40
363.68	80	17.60
409.14	90	19.80
454.60	100	22.00
Litres		U.S.Gallons
3.79	1	0.26
7.57	2	0.53
11.36	3	0.79
15.14	4	1.06
18.93	5	1.32
22.71	6	1.59
26.50	7	1.85
30.28	8	2.11
34.07	9	2.38
37.85	10	2.64
75.71	20	5.28
113.56	30	7.92
151.41	40	10.56
189.27	50	13.21
227.12	60	15.85
264.97	70	18.49
302.82	80	21.13
340.68	90	23.78
378.53	100	26.42

Index

Index

ACKNOWLEDGEMENTS

Philip Clark Limited would like to thank the following for their help in the preparation of this book: M. Jean Bourgeois for all his assistance in contacting people and organizations in France, for reading the text and for his many helpful suggestions; Tom Byers and Wine Buyers Guides Limited for unfailing help and advice; the French Government Tourist Office; Food and Wine from France Limited; Tony Raven for his help in preparing the Index; and Katia Cruft and Helen White for word-processing the manuscript.